Investing for Beginners

Safe, Stress-Free Wealth Building with Index Funds Without Risky Stock Gambling

Ryan Papadopoulos

Disclaimer

This is for educational purposes only. It is not financial, legal, or tax advice. Every person's situation is unique, and you should consider consulting with a licensed professional before making financial decisions. Investing involves risk, including the possible loss of principal. The strategies described here are designed to simplify investing and provide general frameworks, but no outcome is guaranteed. The responsibility for financial decisions remains with you.

Acknowledgments

This was written for everyone who ever felt that money was too complicated, too risky, or out of reach. To the readers who stuck with these pages, thank you for trusting me to guide you. I'm grateful to the people who shared their stories of struggle and success, which shaped the examples you read here. Thanks also to the friends and mentors who pushed me to cut the jargon and keep things honest, practical, and human. And finally, to the ordinary investors—the people who keep showing that small steps, taken consistently, create extraordinary results—you are the reason this book exists.

The Money Boogeyman

You've been lied to. Not in the "aliens built the pyramids" way, but in the quiet, everyday way that makes people freeze when they hear the word investing. Somewhere between the Wall Street movies, your uncle's sketchy "crypto tips," and that news anchor yelling about markets crashing, the message got planted: investing is a rigged game, and you're the sucker at the table.

Here's the truth: the real scam isn't investing. The scam is how complicated people make it look. The jargon, the suits, the scrolling red and green numbers—they all exist to make regular folks feel like they're too dumb to play. That's how Wall Street justifies charging you champagne prices for what is basically tap water.

Let me tell you about my friend Nate. Smart guy, decent job, always quick with a joke. One Thanksgiving, he leaned over his plate of stuffing and whispered like he was handing me state secrets: "Dude, this coin is going to the moon." He was talking about some no-name cryptocurrency. Fast-forward six months: his moon turned out to be a pothole. His $2,000 investment had shriveled to less than what he spent on holiday gifts. That's the kind of story people remember—not because Nate was dumb, but because the game is built to lure you into hype while hiding the boring, reliable stuff that actually works.

I wrote this book because you don't need to gamble to build wealth. You don't need to memorize Greek letters or shout "buy!" into a headset. You don't even need more than a couple hours to set up a system that quietly grows your money while you go about your life.

This book is not about getting rich quick. It's about never being broke again. It's about building stress-free wealth without the constant panic that you're one meme stock away from disaster. By the time you're done, you'll know how to spot scams before they spot you, how to open the exact accounts you need (without the headache), and how to let compounding do the heavy lifting while you binge your favorite show.

If you came here for hype, you're in the wrong place. If you came here for clarity, relief, and a game plan you can actually use? You've just found it. Think of me as your slightly sarcastic friend at the bar—the one who explains money without making you feel like an idiot, occasionally roasts your bad habits, and then hands you a plan that actually works.

Ready? Good. Let's put the money boogeyman back in the closet where he belongs.

Why Everyone's Terrified of Investing (And Why You Don't Have to Be)

My buddy once told me investing was basically Vegas with worse cocktails. He's half right—the drinks are definitely worse. But the game? Not even close. The fear people carry around investing is as heavy as student loans and just as unnecessary. This chapter is about dragging those fears into the light, poking them with a stick, and proving they're not nearly as scary as they look.

The Casino Myth is the biggest one. People think the stock market is just a massive slot machine where you pull a lever and pray. Wall Street loves this misconception because if investing feels like gambling, you'll happily pay them to play for you. They'll package up their "expertise" in fancy suits and jargon, selling you a sense of safety while siphoning off fees. But real investing isn't pulling a lever. It's more like buying a farm. You don't freak out every time the corn prices wiggle. You plant, you wait, you harvest. The game is patience, not luck.

Of course, the fear isn't just theoretical. Everyone has their Money Pit Memory. That cousin who bet the house on crypto. That co-worker who day-traded meme stocks during lunch breaks until their account was emptier than the office snack cabinet. My cousin Chad—God bless him—was one of them. He bought Dogecoin when Elon Musk tweeted a joke, doubled his money in two days, then sat there like a king waiting for his yacht to arrive. Two weeks later, the yacht had sunk, and so had his savings. Stories like this spread like wildfire, convincing regular people that investing equals losing. But what they don't see are the quiet wins—the boring index investor who ignored the noise and doubled their net worth over a decade. The gambler makes headlines. The patient investor retires early.

Then there are the Trust Issues. You're not crazy for being suspicious. The financial world has more scams than a late-night infomercial. Bernie Madoff stole billions by pretending to be a genius. More recently, FTX collapsed faster than a folding chair at a family reunion, taking ordinary people's money with it. Advisors who swear they're fiduciaries sometimes turn out to be salespeople with better hair gel. The system thrives on confusion because confusion is profitable. If you've ever frozen at the idea of investing because you felt the deck was stacked against you, that's not your fault. That's exactly how the system wants you to feel.

But what safe growth really looks like is the exact opposite of the casino floor. It's compounding. It's watching your money reproduce quietly in the background, like leftovers molding in the fridge. You don't notice it at first, but one day you open the door and it's exploded into something unrecognizable. Imagine a graph that's flat as Kansas for years, then suddenly shooting up like Everest. That's the curve of compounding interest. Boring, steady contributions stack on top of each other until they transform into something massive. The trick is time, not luck. And the sooner you start, the steeper the climb.

Here's the Aha Promise: this book isn't here to sell you a lottery ticket. It's here to hand you a map. By the time you've turned the last page, you'll have the tools to explain money to your uncle at Thanksgiving without getting laughed at. You'll have word-for-word scripts to shut down "the next big thing" pitches. You'll have the clarity to see through hype and the confidence to invest without feeling like you're walking into a casino. Investing doesn't have to be scary. It can actually be boring—and that's the secret superpower.

And let's not forget Your Brain vs. Your Money. Fear, FOMO, and loss aversion aren't character flaws—they're baked into our wiring. Humans hate losing twice as much as they love winning. That's why a red number in your account feels like a gut punch, while a green number feels like a shrug. Fear keeps people stuck. FOMO drives them into bad decisions. Markets crash, emotions spike, and we self-sabotage. But here's the relief: you're not dumb. You're just human. Later in this book, I'll hand you mental armor to fight FOMO and calm your nerves during volatility. For now, just know that the instincts making you nervous are the same instincts that kept your ancestors alive. Great for running from tigers, terrible for handling 401(k)s.

So if investing has always felt like a haunted house full of jump scares, it's time to flip on the lights. Behind the smoke machines and scary music, it's just a hallway with a couple of creaky boards. You don't have to gamble. You don't have to guess. You just have to learn the real rules of the game—rules that put boring, patient growth on your side. And once you do, the fear that's been riding shotgun every time you hear the word "investing" will finally shut up and take a backseat.

The Casino Myth

Walk into a casino and you know what you're getting yourself into. Flashing lights, free drinks, a thousand tiny ways to trick your brain into forgetting math. The entire place is designed to drain your wallet with a smile. Somewhere along the way, investing got shoved into the same mental category. People think buying a stock is no different than pulling the handle on a slot machine. Wall Street has done a spectacular job of encouraging that comparison, because the scarier investing feels, the more they can charge you to do it on your behalf.

The truth is that real investing couldn't be further from gambling. Gambling is zero-sum. For you to win, someone else has to lose. The casino always tilts the odds in its favor, so in the long run the house wins and the players limp away lighter. Investing is the opposite. When you buy shares of a company, you're not pulling a lever, you're literally owning a piece of a business. If that business grows, your piece grows. It doesn't require luck, just time. The profits come from the economy expanding, not from fleecing another poor soul across the table.

The confusion sticks because Wall Street dresses itself up in the same kind of spectacle. Instead of spinning roulette wheels, you've got CNBC anchors breathlessly announcing market swings like it's the Super Bowl. Instead of neon lights, you've got scrolling tickers, red and green arrows, and acronyms designed to intimidate. It looks like chaos, so people assume chaos is the point. But beneath the noise, the long-term story of investing is calm, consistent growth that rewards patience, not dice rolls.

Think about it this way: a gambler throws money at chance. An investor plants money in soil. The gambler walks away broke more often than not. The investor waits while the seed quietly becomes a tree. Wall Street profits from making you believe the casino story, because if you think it's all chaos and luck, you'll cling to experts who promise to guide you through. Those experts then charge you hefty fees while quietly parking your money in the same boring index funds you could've bought yourself for pennies.

Let me roast the casino comparison with an example. A guy spends a weekend in Vegas, pulls slots, wins some, loses more, and by Sunday he's down two grand. That's his reality. Meanwhile, someone else puts that same two grand into an S&P 500 index fund and ignores it for ten years. What happens? Historically, that person walks away with closer to four or five grand, depending on the decade. No neon lights, no cocktails, no Elvis impersonators. Just quiet growth doing its thing in the background. The gambler's story ends in regret. The investor's ends in compounding wealth.

The casino myth is sticky because it's simple. People understand the risk of gambling: you lose quickly. That clarity makes it easy to believe investing is just a fancier version with suits instead of dealers. But investing's magic is the opposite of quick. It's built on slowness. That slowness is boring, which means it doesn't make headlines. Nobody tweets about holding the same index fund for thirty years. But they should, because that's the real jackpot.

So if you've been equating the stock market to blackjack, it's time to retire that analogy. The casino is built to distract you while it empties your wallet. Investing is built to quietly reward you for patience and consistency. They may look similar from a distance—money going in, uncertain outcomes coming out—but one is a flashing trap, and the other is a long, boring escalator upward. The trick is stepping on the escalator and staying there, no matter how many flashing lights you see off to the side. Once you get that difference, the fear that investing is just glorified gambling starts to fade. And when that fear fades, you're finally free to see investing for what it is: not a bet, but a partnership with the future.

The Money Pit Memory

Every beginner has at least one scar story. Sometimes it's their own, sometimes it's a relative's, but it always hangs around like a ghost that whispers, "Don't trust investing, you'll lose everything." These stories are powerful because they're emotional. Nobody remembers the friend who quietly doubled their money over ten years in an index fund. Everyone remembers cousin Chad who threw rent money into a shiny new coin, only to watch it evaporate faster than cheap champagne bubbles.

Chad's Dogecoin saga is legendary in my family. One Elon Musk tweet and Chad was convinced he was on the launchpad to billionaire status. He opened an app, tossed in two grand, and checked his phone like a nervous lottery player every hour. At first, the numbers went up. He strutted around at Thanksgiving telling everyone he'd cracked the code of money. But the rocket ran out of fuel. Within weeks, his balance dropped so low it looked like a misprint. When the family asked about his crypto empire the next year, he changed the subject to football.

Stories like Chad's stick because they hit the two emotions that drive money decisions: greed and fear. Greed pulls people in, fear keeps them away afterward. If you've ever thought about investing and then heard a tale of someone losing their shirt in a market plunge, that fear story becomes your brain's default wallpaper. It's easier to remember disasters than boring wins, because disasters are dramatic. That drama cements the myth that investing is a money pit.

But let's untangle what really happens in these cautionary tales. Most "I lost it all" stories involve speculation, not investing. They involve betting on a single stock, or timing the market, or following hype into something nobody really understands. That's not long-term investing—it's gambling dressed up in a different outfit. Of course those stories end badly. They're built on chasing quick wins instead of building slow ones.

Real investing doesn't look like a casino binge or a meme-stock rally. It looks like setting money into a fund that spreads it across hundreds or thousands of companies, then leaving it alone. It looks like boring, automatic deposits that don't make great dinner-table stories. When someone invests that way, they don't become folklore. They just become wealthy quietly, without drama. And because nobody brags about boring wins, the loudest stories we hear are always the disasters.

Thanksgiving dinners are perfect breeding grounds for these fear stories. One relative swears his coworker lost everything in 2008. Another insists they knew a guy who "almost made it" in penny stocks before the rug got pulled. If you don't have the tools to respond, you just sit there, stuffing turkey in your mouth and absorbing the idea that investing equals catastrophe. That's why I like arming readers with what I call the Thanksgiving Clapback Script. It goes something like this: when Uncle Jerry starts in with, "My buddy lost fifty grand in day-trading," you smile, sip your drink, and say, "That's wild, Uncle Jerry. I'm doing the opposite. I put a little into index funds every month, ignore the noise, and I'll be twice as comfortable in twenty years." Then you go back to your mashed potatoes while he tries to process the idea that wealth doesn't have to be flashy or risky.

The danger of Money Pit Memories is that they freeze people before they even start. They take someone who could have built financial stability and convince them that it's safer to do nothing. But doing nothing isn't neutral. Inflation quietly eats at your savings, and opportunities compound away without you. The real pit isn't investing—it's letting fear stories keep you on the sidelines.

What matters is recognizing the pattern. Hot tips, meme frenzies, and viral coins make for entertaining headlines and terrible strategies. They create scars that echo through families and communities, scaring off people who could have thrived by sticking to something steady. Once you see that distinction—between speculation that collapses and investing that compounds—you can put those ghost stories in their proper place. They're not warnings about investing itself. They're warnings about mistaking gambling for investing.

So the next time someone waves their cautionary tale in your face, nod politely, then remember: your path doesn't have to look like theirs. Their money pit is not your destiny. Your plan can be boring, predictable, and ultimately far more rewarding. And boring, in this case, is the best story of all.

Trust Issues

If money had a relationship status with the average person, it would read: "It's complicated." Decades of scams, hype, and so-called advisors who were really just salespeople have left people suspicious, and honestly, they're not wrong. You don't have to be paranoid to think the system is built to confuse you. In fact, confusion is the product. The less you understand, the more someone else can charge you for "help."

Take Bernie Madoff. His entire empire was smoke and mirrors, but because he looked like a respectable Wall Street statesman, people handed him their savings. He stole billions. That kind of betrayal leaves scars that ripple through generations. Fast forward to more recent disasters—FTX collapsed practically overnight, and millions of ordinary people saw their accounts vanish while the company's founder insisted everything was fine. These headlines do more damage than just financial losses; they seed distrust in anyone who dares to touch the word investing.

And it's not just the headline scandals. Walk into a local bank or brokerage, and you'll probably meet an advisor in a crisp suit who smiles warmly while sliding papers across the desk. What most people don't realize is that many of those advisors are incentivized to push products with high fees. They get commissions while you get stuck with hidden costs that quietly eat away at your returns. It's like ordering a glass of water and finding out later you paid champagne prices. No wonder people freeze up. When you don't know who's really on your side, the safest move feels like doing nothing at all.

But doing nothing doesn't protect you—it just hands your future to inflation. The fear is understandable, but it's not the whole picture. Not every advisor is shady, not every product is poison, and not every investment is a scam. The trick is learning how to separate the legitimate from the predatory. Once you understand the red flags, you stop being an easy target. The moment you realize most scams rely on confusion, you start spotting the tricks faster than a magician at a kid's birthday party.

The emotional weight here is important: if you've hesitated to invest because of stories like Madoff or FTX, it's not because you're dumb. It's because the entire industry is built to make you feel out of your depth. That confusion is profitable for them. For you, it's paralyzing. And that paralysis can cost you years of growth that you'll never get back. You're not alone in feeling skeptical. You're just playing on a field where the rules were designed to benefit someone else.

Let's put it plainly. Trust issues with money are rational. Wall Street has earned the skepticism. But skepticism doesn't mean avoidance. It means sharpening your radar so you can tell the difference between a safe, boring index fund and a dressed-up scam. It means questioning advice that comes wrapped in jargon or pressure. It means recognizing that if something sounds too good to be true, it probably is. The relief comes from realizing that you don't have to hand over control of your money to someone who talks fast and wears cufflinks. You can learn the basics yourself, keep your money in vehicles designed to grow steadily, and sleep at night knowing you're not feeding the machine.

The system may be confusing by design, but clarity is possible. Once you see that investing doesn't have to mean trusting shady characters or falling for hype, the fear softens. The rigged-game feeling fades when you realize the game only feels rigged if you're playing by their rules. Change the rules—keep it simple, low-cost, and transparent—and suddenly you're not the sucker at the table anymore. You're the one quietly building wealth while the scammers run out of marks. That shift in perspective is the start of breaking free from the money trust issues that have held so many people back.

What Safe Growth Really Looks Like

When people hear the word growth, they think fireworks. They expect sudden leaps, jackpot moments, dramatic headlines. Real wealth doesn't look like that. Safe growth is quiet, almost invisible in the short term, and then astonishing in the long run. It's the kind of progress you don't brag about at a party because there's nothing flashy to say, but it's the kind that makes you the only one at that same party who retires comfortably while everyone else is still working.

The easiest way to picture safe growth is to think about leftovers in the back of your fridge. On day one, nothing much happens. On day three, maybe there's a spot of fuzz. A week later, it's multiplying like it has a life of its own. Compounding works the same way. Interest, dividends, reinvested earnings—they all start small, almost invisible, until they begin stacking on top of each other. That stack grows faster and faster until what looked flat suddenly curves upward like a roller coaster track. Economists call it exponential growth, but you don't need a math degree to understand it. All you need is patience.

Safe growth thrives on time, not timing. If you drop a few hundred dollars into an account and expect it to double by next summer, you're still thinking like a gambler. If you set that same money to grow over ten, twenty, or thirty years, you're letting compounding do its quiet work. Imagine dropping $100 into an investment every month. For the first year, it feels like nothing special—you've barely saved more than a new phone costs. Ten years in, it's transformed into a down payment on a house. By retirement, it's a nest egg large enough to make your future self wonder how on earth small monthly chunks turned into something so massive. That's safe growth in action.

To see it more clearly, think of a graph. The early years are like Kansas—flat, unremarkable, boring. Stick with it long enough, and the line takes a sharp upward turn, climbing like Everest. That bend in the curve is where compounding stops being background noise and starts being life-changing. People who quit early never see the mountain. They give up while it's still Kansas and assume nothing's happening. But the patient ones, the ones who let time do its thing, they ride that climb without lifting a finger beyond their regular contributions.

What makes this kind of growth safe isn't just the math; it's the mindset. Safe growth doesn't demand constant attention. You don't have to check your balance every day or jump in and out of positions. In fact, that's the danger. Constant tinkering pulls you back into gambler territory. Safe growth asks you to do the opposite: automate, ignore, and let boredom become your ally. It's like planting an orchard. You don't dig up the trees every week to see how the roots are doing. You water them, walk away, and years later you're standing in the shade eating fruit.

Skeptics always ask, what about crashes? What about 2008, or the pandemic, or whatever the next disaster will be? Safe growth accounts for that. Markets dip, sometimes hard, but historically they've always recovered and climbed higher. The dips are temporary; the compounding is permanent. Those who panic-sell lock in losses. Those who ride it out are rewarded. Safe growth isn't about avoiding storms; it's about sailing through them knowing the horizon is still there.

And here's the emotional payoff: once you grasp what safe growth really looks like, the fear of losing everything starts to shrink. It's not a lottery ticket. It's not a trapdoor. It's a long, steady escalator that sometimes jolts but always keeps moving upward. The only way off is if you jump.

So picture your money like mold in the fridge or trees in an orchard—quiet, consistent, multiplying when you're not paying attention. That's what safe growth really looks like. It's not exciting in the moment, but it's the kind of boring that makes you rich. And once you see that clearly, you stop craving the fireworks and start trusting the slow burn that actually works.

The Aha Promise

Every good journey starts with a moment where you realize things don't have to be the way you thought they were. In investing, that moment comes when you finally see that wealth isn't about luck, gambling, or guessing right before everyone else. It's about following a simple path that anyone can walk if they stick with it. That's the promise of this book: to hand you a system that lowers your stress, raises your confidence, and helps your money grow without turning you into a nervous wreck glued to stock tickers.

Most beginners walk into this world bracing for pain. They expect jargon, endless charts, and the smug smirk of someone who seems smarter just because they're wearing cufflinks. That fear becomes a wall, and people avoid even starting. The promise here is that by the time you finish, you won't just understand the basics—you'll know exactly what to do, step by step, and you'll have the words to defend your choices to anyone who tries to push you toward risky nonsense. Relief comes not from hype but from clarity.

Let's be blunt. If you want lottery odds, Vegas is waiting. If you want to build stress-free wealth, this book is going to hand you the playbook. It's not a motivational pep talk. It's not a collection of vague ideas. It's a tool kit. Inside are scripts you can use on the phone with your bank, examples of portfolios that work even for small budgets, and frameworks for shutting down scams before they sink their hooks into you. By the end, you'll have something most people never get: control. Not the illusion of control that comes from chasing hot tips, but the calm control of knowing your plan is solid even when the world feels chaotic.

Imagine yourself at Thanksgiving dinner. Uncle Jerry starts lecturing about the next hot stock, pounding the table with conviction. You don't sweat. You don't argue. You just smile and say, "That's interesting, Jerry. I've set up automatic contributions into an index fund every month. It's simple, reliable, and I don't lose sleep over it." That's your defense script. You don't have to out-debate anyone. You just have to know what you're doing and trust it. That's the aha moment—realizing that confidence doesn't come from predicting the future but from following a plan built to work no matter what.

This promise is also about freedom. Right now, money probably feels like a constant source of stress, an invisible weight that makes you second-guess every decision. By the end, money becomes background noise. It's not gone, but it's not screaming at you. The plan is running on autopilot, and you're free to focus on things that actually matter—your family, your hobbies, your life. The real win here isn't just numbers on a screen; it's the relief of knowing you're okay.

And here's where it gets powerful. Once you see that you don't need to gamble or obsess, you can't unsee it. That's the aha promise. You'll leave this book not just with knowledge but with tools that change how you act. You'll have confidence in conversations, clarity in your accounts, and a new perspective on risk that cuts through the noise. Investing stops being a boogeyman and becomes a quiet ally.

So the promise is simple: clarity over confusion, tools over hype, peace over panic. By the last page, you'll be able to look at your financial future without flinching. You'll have the confidence to ignore the noise and the tools to keep building, one boring, steady step at a time. That's the moment this chapter is leading you toward. That's the promise you'll collect when you stick with me through the rest of the book.

Your Brain vs. Your Money

If you've ever panicked after seeing your account balance dip or felt the urge to jump on a hot trend because everyone else seemed to be getting rich, congratulations—you're human. Your brain is wired to protect you from danger, but when it comes to money, that wiring often backfires. The same instincts that kept your ancestors alive on the savanna are the ones that make you sweat when your portfolio sneezes. To invest well, you don't need a different brain; you just need to understand how yours tricks you and how to outsmart it.

One of the biggest culprits is loss aversion. Psychologists have proven that losing a dollar hurts about twice as much as gaining a dollar feels good. That's why a red number in your account makes your stomach drop, even if the bigger picture is fine. Your brain magnifies losses until they feel catastrophic, and in that panic you're tempted to sell at the worst possible time. Markets dip, you freak out, you sell, then they recover without you. The loss wasn't in the market—it was in your reaction.

Then there's fear of missing out, FOMO. It's the voice that whispers, "Everyone else is getting rich without you." You see friends posting about their crypto wins, or hear coworkers bragging about doubling their money on some stock you've never heard of. FOMO doesn't care about logic. It's a primal itch to belong, to not be left behind by the tribe. But in investing, FOMO lures you into buying high, just before the hype collapses. The crash doesn't just cost you money; it costs you confidence, making you hesitant to invest at all.

Our brains also crave patterns. We love to think we can predict what comes next if we just look hard enough. That's why people obsess over charts with lines and candles that seem to signal hidden truths. But markets don't move in neat, predictable cycles you can read like tarot cards. The urge to see patterns is your brain's survival system misfiring, convincing you there's order in randomness.

Acting on those false patterns often means trading too much, chasing illusions instead of letting compounding work.

It's easy to feel dumb when you fall for these traps, but none of this is about intelligence. It's about biology. We evolved to avoid threats, not to optimize 401(k) balances. When you understand that, you can stop beating yourself up and start building defenses. You can learn to expect that fear and greed will tug at you, and you can design a plan that keeps you from acting on those impulses.

The relief is knowing you don't have to outthink the market. You just have to outthink your instincts. That might mean automating contributions so you can't back out when fear spikes. It might mean setting rules, like only checking your account once a month, so you don't ride the emotional roller coaster of daily fluctuations. It might mean having a script ready for when your friend brags about their latest "win," something as simple as: "Cool. I'm focused on my long-term plan." Short, calm, and confidence-protecting.

Later in this book, you'll get tools that act like armor against FOMO and fear. You'll see how rebalancing, automatic investing, and boring index funds can keep you safe from your own worst impulses. For now, it's enough to realize that the nervousness you feel isn't proof you're bad with money. It's proof you're human. Your wiring is working exactly as designed—it just wasn't designed for investing.

Once you accept that, the fear loses some of its sting. You stop thinking, "I'm terrible with money," and start thinking, "My brain is playing its old tricks again." That small shift makes it possible to stay calm in the face of volatility and to resist the herd when hype swirls around you. And that calm is where real investing begins. Not with perfect knowledge or crystal-ball predictions, but with the simple ability to sit tight when your instincts scream at you to run.

The Language of Money Without the Jargon

Ever nodded along in a money conversation only to sneak off and Google a term like "P/E ratio" in the bathroom? You're not alone. Financial language has been engineered to sound intimidating, like a secret code you're not supposed to understand. But underneath the acronyms and the alphabet soup, the basics are surprisingly simple. Once you see them clearly, you'll realize that most of the mystery is smoke and mirrors. The fear fades when the words lose their sting.

The first step is stripping the drama away. A stock isn't a monster hiding under the bed. It's just a tiny piece of ownership in a company. If you own Apple stock, you literally own a sliver of Apple. You and millions of strangers are co-owners of one of the biggest companies on the planet. When Apple sells more iPhones, your little slice of the pie gets more valuable. That's it. You're not gambling; you're hitching a ride on the growth of real businesses that make real things. Once you see stocks as slices of pizza rather than lottery tickets, they stop feeling so scary.

Bonds get a bad rap for being boring, but boring is their superpower. A bond is nothing more than a loan. You lend money to a government or a company, and in return, they promise to pay you interest and eventually give your money back. That's it. No glitz, no gamble. Think of bonds as the reliable friend who always pays you back with a little extra for the trouble. They may not deliver fireworks, but they're steady, and steady is underrated when it comes to building wealth.

Then there are index funds, the ultimate cheat code. Imagine wanting to buy one slice of every pizza in the shop so you don't have to pick the perfect one. That's what an index fund does. It buys tiny pieces of hundreds or even thousands of companies at once. Instead of guessing which company will soar, you just ride the whole market. Historically, the whole market has grown over time. Index funds are simple, low-cost, and they remove the pressure of having to be a stock-picking genius. Relief comes the moment you realize you don't need to outsmart Wall Street to win—you just need to stay in the game.

Mutual funds are the cousin of index funds, but they often come with hidden strings. Many are actively managed, which means someone in a suit is picking stocks on your behalf. They charge you high fees for this privilege, fees that eat away at your returns year after year. Imagine paying champagne prices and getting tap water. Over decades, those extra costs can strip away tens of thousands of dollars you could have kept. The takeaway isn't that all mutual funds are evil, but that many are overpriced middlemen when a simple index fund could do the job better.

Exchange-traded funds, or ETFs, are like index funds with a modern twist. They're easy to buy and sell, often through the same apps you'd use for stocks. Think of them as ordering pizza on a Tuesday night with one click. You pick the ETF you want, tap the buy button, and boom—you're invested across a wide range of companies without the fuss. They combine the diversification of index funds with the convenience of stocks, making them one of the most beginner-friendly tools out there.

The real breakthrough here is realizing that none of these terms are as scary as they sound. Stocks, bonds, index funds, ETFs—they're just different flavors of the same basic idea: putting your money to work so it grows over time. Once you see through the jargon, you stop feeling excluded from the club. You don't need an MBA or a Wall Street badge to get it. You just need plain explanations and a willingness to ignore the hype.

By the end of this chapter, you should feel lighter. The words that used to sound like traps are just labels on simple concepts. Owning companies, lending money, buying baskets of both—it's not complicated, it's just dressed up to look that way. Strip off the costume, and the language of money becomes as straightforward as ordering dinner. And when the words lose their power to intimidate, the whole game of investing starts to look a lot less sc

Stocks Aren't Monsters

For most beginners, the word "stock" triggers the same nerves as hearing a strange noise in the middle of the night. You picture risk, chaos, maybe even disaster. That fear is partly cultural—Wall Street dramas on TV, news clips of traders screaming at each other, headlines about crashes—but mostly it's because nobody ever sat you down and explained what a stock actually is. When you strip away the theatrics, a stock is one of the simplest financial tools you'll ever meet. It's not a monster. It's a slice of ownership in a business, and that business grows whether you check your account or not.

Owning a stock means you are literally a shareholder. Picture a giant pizza. The company is the pizza, and the shares are slices. Each slice entitles you to a portion of the profits. When the company sells more products, expands into new markets, or simply gets better at making money, the value of the whole pizza rises—and so does your slice. That's all there is to it. You're not placing a bet on the roulette wheel; you're partnering with a business to share in its success.

The misconception that stocks are wild gambles comes from focusing on the short term. Yes, in a week or even a year, a stock price can swing up and down like a roller coaster. Those swings feel like danger because we're hardwired to see volatility as risk. But stretch out the timeline, and the picture changes completely. Companies that grow steadily tend to make their shareholders richer over the long run, no matter how bumpy the ride looked in between. Think about Apple. If you bought shares twenty years ago, the day-to-day dips and spikes would have been distracting, but the long-term climb would have turned a modest investment into life-changing money.

You might already own stocks without realizing it. If you have a retirement plan through work, like a 401(k), there's a good chance part of your paycheck has been buying stocks for years. Millions of ordinary people own little chunks of big companies this way. They don't spend their days glued to financial news. They just contribute regularly and let time do its work. That realization alone—that you may already be an investor—can shift your perspective from fear to familiarity.

To understand why stocks grow in value, remember that companies exist to make profits. They design products, provide services, and earn money. As those profits accumulate, investors are willing to pay more for shares. On top of that, many companies share a portion of their profits directly with shareholders in the form of dividends. That means you're not just betting on a future payoff—you can earn income along the way simply by holding the stock.

This is where beginners get stuck: the fear of picking the wrong stock. Nobody wants to choose the slice that ends up burned at the bottom of the oven. And yes, choosing individual companies can be risky if you put all your money in one place. Businesses fail. Trends shift. That's why diversification exists. Instead of buying one slice, you can spread your money across the whole pizza shop—or even the entire restaurant industry—by using index funds or ETFs. But the core point remains: a stock itself isn't dangerous. The danger comes from misunderstanding how to use it.

Think of stocks as tools. A hammer can build a house or smash a window—it depends on how you use it. Stocks can be vehicles for long-term wealth or tickets to stress city, depending on whether you chase quick wins or settle in for the long haul. Once you see them as simple slices of businesses rather than mysterious beasts, the fear fades. The monster under the bed turns out to be just a shadow.

So the next time you hear someone talk about "the stock market" like it's a casino, remember the pizza. Remember that companies grow by selling products and making profits, and owning a stock ties you to that growth. The noise, the headlines, the daily drama—that's just the surface. Underneath, it's as straightforward as being one of many co-owners of a business. Once you understand that, stocks stop being scary and start looking like what they really are: your ticket to ride the wave of economic growth.

Bonds: The Boring Heroes

If stocks are the flashy kids at school—the ones making headlines, pulling stunts, and getting everyone's attention—then bonds are the quiet honor-roll students who never cause trouble but always get the job done. Bonds don't grab the spotlight, and they're rarely the star of a dinner-table brag. But when it comes to building steady, reliable wealth, they are the unsung heroes.

At their core, bonds are simply loans. You lend your money to a government or a company, and in return, they promise to pay you back with interest. That's it. No bells, no whistles, no neon signs. Just a straightforward agreement: you provide the cash now, they return it later with a thank-you payment attached. Unlike stocks, where your returns depend on how profitable a company becomes, bonds spell out exactly what you'll receive and when. That predictability is what makes them powerful.

Think about lending money to a friend who always pays you back on time. It might not be thrilling, but it's dependable. Bonds are like that, except your friend is more likely to be the U.S. government or a massive corporation than your neighbor down the street. When you buy a government bond, you're essentially lending Uncle Sam a chunk of change so he can keep the lights on. In return, you get interest payments and the promise that your money comes back at the end of the bond's term. It's not glamorous, but it works.

The reputation of bonds as "boring" is exactly why they matter. Boring means stability. Boring means less drama when markets swing up and down. When stocks crash and investors are panicking, bonds are often the safety net that cushions the fall. They don't eliminate risk entirely—companies can default, governments can stumble—but compared to the roller coaster of stock prices, bonds are the part of your portfolio that lets you sleep at night.

There's also an emotional edge here. For beginners, bonds provide comfort. Watching a steady interest payment arrive feels different from riding the volatility of stocks. Bonds remind you that not every investment has to feel like a storm. They balance the noise, offering calm in a sea of uncertainty. They are like ballast in a ship, keeping it steady when the waves get rough. Without them, a portfolio can feel unhinged, tossing with every gust of market wind.

Of course, bonds aren't perfect. The biggest trade-off is that they generally grow more slowly than stocks. If stocks are the sprint, bonds are the slow, steady walk. But that walk has value. Imagine being near retirement and knowing you can count on a predictable stream of income. Imagine weathering a market downturn and having a portion of your money shielded from the chaos. That kind of reliability isn't just financial—it's psychological. It keeps you from panicking and making bad decisions in stressful times.

Bonds also come in different flavors. Treasury bonds from the U.S. government are about as safe as it gets, because Uncle Sam has never defaulted. Corporate bonds carry a bit more risk, but they pay higher interest to make up for it. Municipal bonds help fund schools, roads, and public projects, while offering tax benefits. Each type has its place, but the key is that they all follow the same basic principle: you lend, you earn interest, you get your money back.

And let's clear up one common mix-up: no, a bond doesn't mean James Bond is swooping in to save your portfolio. The only thing these bonds are rescuing is your sense of stability. They aren't glamorous, they don't carry martinis or Aston Martins, but they do give your investments balance. In a world obsessed with fast profits and flashy headlines, bonds stand out precisely because they don't chase drama.

So while stocks may get all the glory, bonds deserve your respect. They are the boring heroes in the background, doing the steady work of protecting your portfolio from extremes. When combined with stocks, they create a balance that makes long-term investing not just profitable but sustainable. They're the friend who shows up on time, every time, and quietly helps you win in the long run.

Index Funds: The Cheat Code

If there's a single idea that has rescued more ordinary people from financial confusion than any other, it's the index fund. For beginners, it feels almost unfair, like discovering a video game cheat code after struggling for hours. While everyone else is sweating over which stock to buy, how to time the market, or whether their advisor is worth the fees, you can sidestep the whole circus with one move: buy the whole market at once.

An index fund is a basket that holds tiny pieces of many companies. Instead of betting on which business will skyrocket and which will flop, you buy them all together. If the economy grows, the basket grows. You're not putting your eggs in one basket—you're putting one egg in every basket and letting the farm expand. The idea is so simple it almost feels like cheating, which is why seasoned investors like Warren Buffett repeatedly recommend index funds to beginners and even to their own families.

What makes index funds magical isn't just diversification—it's the low cost. Wall Street has built an empire convincing people they need to pay high fees for experts to pick stocks. The dirty secret is that most experts don't beat the market over time. They shuffle money around, look busy, and collect fat fees while the average investor lags behind. Index funds skip the middleman. They track the market automatically, which means there's no highly paid manager draining your returns. Over decades, that difference in fees can add up to hundreds of thousands of dollars staying in your pocket instead of someone else's.

Imagine this in practice. You open an investing app, type in the ticker symbol for a broad index fund—something that covers the entire U.S. stock market or the S&P 500—and click buy. That's it. In a single move, you've invested in hundreds or thousands of companies, from giants like Apple and Amazon to smaller businesses you've never heard of. If one company stumbles, it barely matters, because the others carry the weight. You've spread your risk so wide that no single disaster can sink you.

There's an emotional payoff here too. Index funds take away the pressure of trying to be a genius. You don't need to spend nights reading financial statements or mornings chasing headlines. You don't need to guess which industry will dominate next decade. You simply ride the collective growth of businesses across the economy. That relief—that sudden exhale when you realize you don't have to play the stock-picking game—is the aha moment many people feel the first time they learn about index funds.

Skeptics sometimes complain that index funds are boring. They don't have the thrill of a big win on a single stock. But that so-called boredom is exactly what makes them powerful. Instead of adrenaline, you get peace of mind. Instead of drama, you get consistency. And consistency, over decades, compounds into results that most gamblers never achieve. The bragging rights may not arrive tomorrow, but twenty years from now, you'll be the one enjoying freedom while the thrill-seekers are still chasing losses.

Think of it like a buffet. You could try to guess which dish will be best and risk being disappointed, or you could take a little of everything and be sure you won't go hungry. Index funds are the buffet table of investing. They guarantee you get the average performance of the market—which, historically, has been very good—without the stress of betting your future on a single plate.

So when you hear the phrase "index fund," don't let the jargon scare you. Translate it into what it really means: safety through variety, growth through patience, and peace through simplicity. It's the cheat code that turns investing from a confusing gamble into a straightforward plan. And once you see how easy it is, you'll wonder why anyone still pays for the privilege of playing a harder, riskier game.

Why Mutual Funds Often Suck

For decades, mutual funds were sold as the default choice for anyone who wanted to invest but didn't want to pick individual stocks. The pitch sounded great: "Hand your money to a professional manager, let them make the tough calls, and watch your savings grow." On the surface, it feels safe—someone smart is steering the ship while you sit back. But when you peel back the glossy brochures and the polished sales pitches, you find a lot of hidden problems. Mutual funds often deliver champagne prices for tap water, and most beginners never realize it until years of returns have been eaten alive by fees.

Here's the ugly truth: most mutual funds are actively managed. That means a manager and their team are constantly buying and selling stocks in an attempt to beat the market. Sounds good, right? Except study after study has shown that the vast majority of them fail to outperform the simple alternative: index funds. They shuffle money around, make a lot of trades, and collect their paychecks, but over the long haul, they lag behind. The rare managers who do outperform are nearly impossible to identify ahead of time. It's like betting on which horse will win not just one race, but every race for the next thirty years. The odds aren't in your favor.

The bigger problem is the fees. Mutual funds often come with layers of costs: management fees, administrative fees, trading costs, and sometimes even sales commissions. These fees might look tiny—maybe one or two percent a year—but over decades, they can gut your returns. Imagine two people investing $10,000 each. One chooses a high-fee mutual fund charging 2% annually, the other chooses a low-cost index fund at 0.1%. After twenty years, the index fund investor could have tens of thousands more than the mutual fund investor, simply because they didn't bleed money to fees. That's not a small difference—it's the difference between retiring comfortably and working extra years to catch up.

Mutual funds also limit your flexibility. They only trade once per day, at the closing price. That may not sound like a big deal, but it means you don't get the convenience or transparency you'd find in an ETF or index fund you can buy and sell instantly. It reinforces the feeling that you're handing control over to someone else, and you just have to hope they're doing a good job.

Then there's the marketing machine. Mutual funds are pushed aggressively by banks and brokers because they're profitable—for the institutions, not for you. Glossy ads promise safety and expertise, while the fine print hides the costs. Advisors often get commissions for recommending certain funds, which means their advice might be more about lining their pockets than protecting yours. Beginners don't know to ask about fees or incentives, so they end up paying premium prices for average results.

That's not to say every mutual fund is evil. There are low-cost mutual funds that essentially mimic index funds, and those can be fine. But the majority that beginners stumble into are overpriced and overhyped. The danger isn't just losing money—it's losing time. Every extra dollar that goes into fees is a dollar that doesn't compound for you. Over decades, that lost compounding power adds up to staggering amounts.

The point isn't that mutual funds never work. It's that they rarely justify their costs when simpler, cheaper, and often more effective options exist. You don't need to pay high fees for average performance. You don't need to bankroll someone else's lifestyle just to get access to the market. Once you understand this, the shine wears off quickly. What looked like a polished, professional solution is often just a dressed-up way of siphoning your returns.

So why do mutual funds often suck? Because they promise expertise but deliver mediocrity, and they charge you heavily for the privilege. The smarter move is to keep your money in low-cost, broad-based funds that don't drain your wallet while pretending to outsmart the market. When you realize this, you stop being dazzled by the sales pitch and start keeping more of your hard-earned money where it belongs—with you.

ETFs in Real Life

If index funds are the cheat code, then exchange-traded funds—ETFs—are the cheat code with a turbo button. They take the simplicity of index funds and layer on convenience, making them one of the easiest ways for beginners to start investing without the headaches. The name might sound technical, but in practice, ETFs are as casual as ordering a pizza on a Tuesday night. You pick the one you want, tap buy in your brokerage app, and suddenly you own a slice of hundreds or thousands of companies.

An ETF works a lot like an index fund. It pools together stocks, bonds, or other assets into a single package so you don't have to pick winners and losers. The big difference is flexibility. While mutual funds only trade once a day, ETFs trade all day long, just like individual stocks. That means you can buy or sell whenever you want during market hours. You don't need to wait for some mysterious end-of-day calculation. You see the price, you click, and you're in. That transparency is one reason ETFs have exploded in popularity over the last two decades.

But the real appeal for beginners is how easy they are to use. Open your investing app, search for a ticker symbol, and hit buy. That's it. You don't need to fill out stacks of paperwork or sit through a sales pitch. If you want broad exposure to the U.S. market, you might buy an ETF that tracks the S&P 500. If you want international exposure, there are ETFs for that too. Want a mix of stocks and bonds? There are ETFs designed to give you balanced exposure in a single package. It's investing simplified down to a one-click decision.

Costs are another big win for ETFs. Like index funds, they usually come with very low fees, often fractions of a percent. Compare that to the bloated fees of many mutual funds, and you can see why ETFs are the modern favorite. The less you pay in fees, the more of your money stays invested, compounding over time. That difference may not look dramatic at first, but over decades it translates into thousands of extra dollars in your account instead of someone else's.

ETFs also carry an emotional advantage. Beginners often feel anxious about making the "right" choice, worried they'll pick the wrong stock and watch their money vanish. With ETFs, that fear shrinks because you're instantly diversified. You're not betting on one company to succeed; you're spreading your money across many. If one company stumbles, the others pick up the slack. That built-in safety net gives you confidence to start investing without feeling like you're gambling.

Of course, ETFs aren't perfect. Some are overly complicated, designed to chase trendy themes or exotic strategies. Those are best avoided, especially for beginners. The real strength of ETFs lies in their simplicity—broad, low-cost funds that cover entire markets. The temptation to chase niche ETFs that promise outsized returns is just another version of speculation dressed up in new clothes. Stick with the basics, and you'll get the full benefit without the unnecessary risk.

Explaining ETFs to a friend can be refreshingly simple. You might say, "It's like buying a basket of stocks instead of one stock. Instead of guessing which company will do best, I buy them all at once through an ETF. It costs almost nothing, and I can sell it whenever I want." That kind of plain explanation cuts through the intimidation and shows how accessible investing really is.

The takeaway is that ETFs combine the best features of stocks and index funds. They offer diversification, low costs, and ease of use, all wrapped in a package you can buy with a few taps. They demystify investing by putting the tools directly in your hands without hidden layers of complexity. For beginners, that accessibility is gold. Once you realize how straightforward ETFs are, the fear of starting fades away. What's left is a clear, practical path to building wealth without the noise and drama of Wall Street.

Opening the Gates (How to Actually Start)

Knowing what stocks, bonds, and funds are is one thing. Actually opening your first account is another beast entirely. For most people, the idea of handing over personal details to a faceless website feels like tossing their identity into a black hole. You imagine hackers in hoodies selling your Social Security number on eBay before you've even clicked "submit." That anxiety is normal, but it doesn't have to stop you. Setting up your first account can feel intimidating, yet it's far simpler—and safer—than your fears make it out to be. Once you see the process laid out clearly, you'll wonder why you waited so long.

The first thing to understand is that you need a place for your money to live before it can start working for you. Think of it like a garden: you can't grow anything if you don't have a plot of land. In investing, that land is your account. For most beginners, the choice comes down to either a retirement account, like an IRA, or a regular brokerage account. The IRA comes with tax benefits and long-term restrictions—you're setting money aside for future you. A brokerage account is more flexible; you can take money in and out whenever you want, but you won't get the same tax perks. Neither choice is wrong, but knowing which one fits your goals makes the whole process less scary.

The actual setup is surprisingly straightforward. You go online, pick a reputable brokerage, and fill out a form. It asks for basics—your name, address, Social Security number, employment details. It feels invasive, but it's no different from applying for a bank account. These companies need your information to comply with federal regulations, not because they want to snoop through your life. Once you've entered the details, you set up a username, create a password, and connect your bank account. That's the moment of truth—linking your checking account so you can transfer money in. But here's the secret: the money doesn't vanish into the ether. It just moves into your investment account, ready to be put to work.

For anyone still nervous, picture it like opening a digital wallet that only you can access. The brokerage isn't some shady alleyway vendor. These are regulated institutions that survive on trust. They don't profit by stealing your money—they profit by keeping your account safe and charging small fees on trades or fund expenses. Once you realize that, the fear of pressing "submit" starts to fade.

The emotional shift happens quickly. At first, setting up the account feels like stepping into the unknown. But once you log in and see your account screen for the first time, something changes. The numbers may be zero at the start, but that blank canvas is powerful. It's proof that you've crossed the starting line. You've moved from thinking about investing to actually creating the space for your money to grow. That small step gives you momentum, and momentum is everything.

From there, you can make your first deposit. It doesn't have to be huge—fifty or a hundred dollars is enough. The point isn't to get rich overnight. The point is to get comfortable. Seeing that first transfer hit your account gives you a tangible sense of progress. You're no longer just a saver; you're an investor. That shift in identity is worth more than the dollars in the account, because it changes how you see yourself. You start to believe you belong in the world of investing, not as a guest, but as a participant.

The best part is realizing how little ongoing effort it takes. Once the account is open and funded, you don't have to constantly babysit it. You don't have to log in every day. You've built the foundation, and from here, everything else—choosing funds, automating contributions, setting long-term goals—becomes possible. Without this first step, nothing happens. With it, you've officially opened the gates. The scary part is over, and the path ahead is clear. The account that once felt like a black hole becomes the launchpad for every financial goal you've ever had.

The First Account You'll Ever Love

Your first real investment account is like your first apartment. It may not have granite countertops or a fancy view, but it's yours, and that ownership is what matters. This is where your money starts working instead of just sitting around looking lazy in a savings account. The decision between an IRA and a brokerage account might feel overwhelming at first, but once you strip away the jargon, it's straightforward. An IRA is your retirement apartment—you commit to staying for the long haul, and in return you get tax perks that can save you thousands over the years. A brokerage account is your flexible crash pad—you can come and go as you please, but you won't get the same long-term benefits. Which one you open first depends on your goals, but either way, the act of opening one changes everything.

Picture yourself at your laptop, cursor hovering over the "Open Account" button. Your palms are sweaty like you're about to propose marriage, but what you're really doing is marrying your future self. The forms ask about your name, your Social Security number, your job. It feels uncomfortably personal, but these aren't prying questions—they're requirements to keep your money safe in a highly regulated system. When you hit submit, the website doesn't suck your soul into a void. It sets up a digital container with your name on it, protected by law, where your money will live and grow.

The first account you'll ever love is the one that makes you feel empowered instead of anxious. Think of logging in for the first time like walking into an empty apartment. The walls are bare, but the potential is unlimited. That initial zero balance isn't a failure—it's an invitation. When you move money from your checking account into this space, you're not losing it. You're relocating it to a place where it can finally work on your behalf. The first time you see a deposit show up, no matter how small, you feel the shift. Suddenly you're not just a saver stockpiling cash for emergencies—you're an investor building a future.

This account becomes the foundation of your financial story. With an IRA, you're telling future you, "I've got your back." You're locking money away where it can grow tax-advantaged for decades, compounding quietly while you live your life. With a brokerage account, you're giving yourself flexibility, a sandbox to learn and grow without restrictions. Both choices have value, and many people eventually use both. The key is not perfection—it's progress. Opening one of them means you've stepped out of the audience and onto the stage.

Emotions will try to mess with you here. The setup feels like a big deal because it is. It's the line between thinking about investing and actually doing it. You might hesitate, wondering if you've picked the right type of account or if you should have waited. But here's the truth: the best account is the one you actually open. The details matter less than the action. Once you've started, adjustments can be made. You're not carving your financial future in stone—you're laying down the first brick.

Over time, this first account grows on you. It's the place you check when you need a boost of confidence, the proof that you're moving forward even if progress feels slow. Every contribution adds to that feeling. What began as an intimidating blank page becomes a story you're proud to write. And when you look back years later, you'll remember the nerves, the hesitation, and then the relief. You'll realize that this ordinary-looking account was the first step toward extraordinary freedom.

That's why it becomes the first account you'll ever love. Not because it's glamorous or exciting, but because it's yours. It's the point where you stopped standing on the sidelines and started building. It's the container that holds not just your money, but your commitment to a future where you call the shots.

Scripts for the Phone Call

Once you've opened your first account, the next intimidating hurdle is often the phone call. For some reason, dialing up customer service feels scarier than sending thousands of dollars into cyberspace. You picture yourself stammering, forgetting what to ask, or getting bulldozed by some smooth-talking rep who sounds like they've been doing this since the dawn of time. That fear is normal, but here's the reality: you don't have to wing it. Having a script in your back pocket changes everything. It turns an awkward conversation into a confident step forward.

Picture this: you dial the brokerage number, palms sweaty, already rehearsing your Social Security number like you're cramming for an exam. A friendly voice picks up. Here's where most beginners freeze, blurting out something vague like, "Uh, I want to invest?" That's when the rep launches into jargon and you start drowning. Instead, you walk in prepared.

Here's a confident version of the script:

"Hi, I just opened an account with you, and I want to make sure I'm setting it up correctly. I'd like to confirm that my account is a standard brokerage account (or IRA, if that's what you chose). I'm planning to invest in index funds, and I want to make sure I'm choosing the right options. Can you point me to where I can see the list of available funds and their fees?"

Notice what happens here. You sound calm, clear, and in control. You're not asking them to design your portfolio. You're simply directing the conversation, confirming your account type, and making sure you know where to look. This frames you as someone who knows what they want, which keeps the rep from trying to upsell you into high-fee nonsense.

Now here's the nervous version of the script, for when you're feeling less like a CEO and more like a deer in headlights:

"Hi, I'm new to this and just opened an account. I'd like to make sure I set it up right. I don't know much about investing, but I've read that index funds are a good place to start. Can you help me find those in your system?"

This version is just as effective. You're admitting you're new, which is fine, but you're also steering the conversation toward what you want: index funds. You're not giving them an opening to suggest exotic products, day-trading tools, or anything that doesn't fit your plan. You're telling them exactly where you want to go, even if you phrase it with humility.

The reason scripts matter is that they take the emotion out of the moment. When you're on the spot, nerves can hijack your brain. With a script, you've already decided the words before you dial. You don't have to scramble. The rep may throw jargon at you, but you can always come back to your line: "I'm focused on index funds with low fees. Can you show me where to find them?" That's your anchor. Repeat it as many times as needed.

This is also where you realize something crucial: customer service reps aren't mystical gatekeepers. They're employees reading from their own scripts. Their job is to help you navigate the system. They don't have secret knowledge you can't access. They can point you to resources, explain how to place an order, and confirm your account details. But you're the one in control of your money, and you set the boundaries of the conversation.

The first time you make that call, it feels monumental. But after it's over, you realize how routine it is. You spoke, you asked for what you needed, and the world didn't end. That boost of confidence carries forward. It's proof that you don't need to be fluent in finance jargon to handle your own accounts. You just need clarity and a few lines in your pocket.

By the time you hang up, you'll notice something unexpected: relief. You've turned what felt like a terrifying step into a straightforward task. That's how you know you're making progress. The phone call wasn't a test you had to ace—it was another brick laid in the foundation of your financial independence.

Password Terror

For all the talk about picking the right funds or opening the right account, the part that trips up most beginners is far less glamorous: the password. It's ridiculous, really. You can make decisions worth thousands of dollars without blinking, but then you freeze when the screen asks you to create a password. Suddenly, you're back in 2005, typing your cat's name followed by 123, hoping no one ever guesses it. The problem is that online accounts are only as safe as the gates you build, and too many people guard their future wealth with something a bored teenager could crack.

This isn't about paranoia. It's about practicality. Your brokerage account isn't just another login like Netflix. It's the digital key to your financial life. If someone breaks in, they won't just watch The Office on your dime—they could siphon off everything you've built. That's why creating a strong, unique password isn't optional. It's the modern equivalent of locking your front door at night.

So what makes a password strong? Not birthdays, not pet names, not anything you'd share on social media. Hackers know people recycle obvious details. A strong password is long, unpredictable, and impossible to guess by someone who knows you. The best way to do this without losing your mind is to use a password manager. Think of it as a digital vault. You only need to remember one master password, and the vault generates and remembers dozens of complex ones for every site you use. That way, your brokerage account isn't relying on "Fluffy123," it's protected by a random string of letters, numbers, and symbols that even you couldn't memorize.

The terror often comes from the idea of forgetting. People imagine locking themselves out of their accounts forever. But password managers are designed to prevent that. They back up securely, sync across devices, and can be recovered with the right steps. The real danger isn't forgetting—it's underestimating the risk of being careless. A stolen Netflix account is annoying. A stolen investment account is devastating.

Security questions add another layer of comedy and risk. "What's your mother's maiden name?" or "What's the name of your first school?" These answers are often easy to find with a quick search or social media scroll. Treat them like extra passwords. Don't answer with the truth—answer with nonsense you'll only remember through your password manager. If the question is "What's your favorite food?" your answer could be "BlueElephantGuitar." Nobody can guess it, and you've turned a weak link into a strong one.

Two-factor authentication is the final piece. When your brokerage offers it, use it. This means that even if someone somehow guesses your password, they still need access to your phone or email to break in. It's like having a deadbolt on top of the lock. Slightly less convenient, yes, but infinitely safer. A few extra seconds to log in is a small price to pay for peace of mind.

The deeper truth here is that good security isn't about living in fear. It's about making smart choices once so you don't have to think about them again. Create a strong password, set up two-factor authentication, and move on. That's it. You don't need to obsess or constantly check if you're safe. You just need to build a solid wall around your account and trust it.

The relief comes when you realize that password terror is temporary. You only have to wrestle with it once. After that, the systems you set up carry the load. Instead of lying awake worrying that someone might guess your pet's name, you can rest knowing your investments are guarded by layers of protection most hackers won't bother to challenge. The fear shrinks, replaced by the calm knowledge that you've taken care of business.

So yes, laugh at the absurdity of sweating over a password. But don't dismiss it. In the hierarchy of financial steps, this one may not be glamorous, but it's foundational. Strong security is what ensures the money you invest stays yours. Conquer password terror once, and it never controls you again.

Direct Deposit = Automatic Investing

There's a moment in every beginner's journey when they realize investing doesn't have to be complicated, dramatic, or stressful. That moment usually comes when they set up automatic investing through direct deposit. It's the closest thing to putting your wealth on autopilot. You don't have to wrestle with temptation, second-guess every move, or remember to transfer money each month. The system simply pulls a portion of your paycheck, sends it into your investment account, and starts building your future while you go about your life. Once it's running, you barely notice it—until years later when you look back and see how much has piled up without effort.

The magic of direct deposit is momentum. Left to our own devices, we procrastinate. We tell ourselves we'll transfer money at the end of the month, but then the car needs repairs, or there's a trip we justify as "once in a lifetime," or we simply forget. The month slips by, and nothing gets invested. With direct deposit, you don't rely on willpower. The system does the remembering for you. Before you have a chance to spend it, the money is gone to a place where it quietly multiplies.

Think of it like brushing your teeth. If you had to decide every night whether to do it, you'd probably skip more than you'd like to admit. But because it's automatic, it's just part of life. Direct deposit creates the same rhythm for your finances. You don't debate, you don't stress—you just build. The habit stacks on itself, and the results show up later in the form of compound growth.

This isn't about giant sums. You don't need to shovel half your paycheck into investments to make progress. Even a small slice—fifty or a hundred dollars a month—adds up. The key is consistency, not size. Imagine setting aside $100 every month starting at age twenty-five. By retirement, that modest habit has turned into hundreds of thousands of dollars, thanks to compounding. You didn't have to time the market. You didn't have to become a financial wizard. You just had to let the system work on schedule.

There's also an emotional shift that comes with automation. At first, the idea of money leaving your paycheck without you touching it feels unnerving, like losing control. But over time, you feel the opposite. You're in control precisely because you're not leaving things to chance. You're deciding once, upfront, to prioritize your future. The peace of mind that comes from knowing the deposits happen no matter what is priceless. It's like hiring a disciplined version of yourself to handle money while the real you enjoys life.

If you're wondering how to set this up, it's usually as simple as filling out a form with your employer or logging into your HR portal. You enter the account number for your brokerage or IRA, decide how much of your paycheck should go there, and that's it. Every pay period, the money flows automatically. If you don't want to reroute your paycheck directly, another option is to set up an automatic transfer from your bank account into your investment account on payday. Either way, you've built a pipeline between earning and investing that requires no ongoing effort.

Here's a script you can literally send to HR if you want to split your paycheck: "Hi, I'd like to deposit $200 from each paycheck into my brokerage account ending in [last four digits]. Can you set up a split direct deposit for me?" Short, clear, and effective. No need to overexplain or apologize. It's your paycheck—you get to decide where it goes.

The biggest win here is psychological. Direct deposit turns investing from a chore into background noise. It stops being something you have to remember and becomes something that just happens. That frees up mental space. You don't have to constantly check if you're "on track" or beat yourself up for forgetting. You can trust the system to handle it, knowing that future you will reap the rewards.

Once you experience the ease of automatic investing, you'll never go back. It transforms wealth-building from an irregular, guilt-ridden task into a calm, consistent process. It's not glamorous, but it's powerful. Over time, those invisible deposits are what make the visible difference between living paycheck to paycheck and stepping into financial freedom.

Mistakes to Dodge on Day One

Starting something new always comes with the risk of rookie errors, and investing is no different. The difference is that these mistakes can cost real money instead of just pride. Luckily, most of them are easy to avoid once you know what they look like. The goal isn't to be perfect on day one—it's to sidestep the most common traps so your account starts off strong and steady rather than wobbly and full of regrets.

The first mistake many beginners make is choosing the wrong type of account. Imagine showing up to the airport with a ticket to the wrong destination. You still get on a plane, but it takes you somewhere you never planned to go. If your long-term goal is retirement, opening a taxable brokerage account instead of an IRA could mean missing out on tax breaks worth thousands of dollars over the years. On the flip side, if you're saving for something shorter-term, like buying a house, tying up all your money in a retirement account can backfire when you want to withdraw. The cure is simple: pause for a moment, decide what you want your money to do, and pick the account type that matches. The setup takes minutes, but the consequences of rushing can last decades.

Another classic blunder is dabbling in margin trading without realizing it. Margin is just a fancy way of saying you're borrowing money from your broker to invest. It might feel like free leverage at first, but it's more like playing with dynamite. Gains are magnified, sure, but so are losses. Many platforms make it dangerously easy to check a box and suddenly you're trading with borrowed cash you never meant to touch. The best defense is to keep it simple: if you're a beginner, margin doesn't exist. Stick to investing only what you actually have, and you'll sleep better at night.

Then there's the panic button problem. Picture a new investor clicking through their brokerage app, curious about all the shiny buttons. One wrong tap, and suddenly they've placed a trade they didn't mean to. It happens more often than you'd think. The excitement of exploring quickly turns into fear when you realize you've just bought 50 shares of something you can't even pronounce. These mistakes are rarely catastrophic if caught quickly, but they highlight the importance of slowing down. Read the screen twice before you click. Your account isn't a video game—there's no reset button.

New investors also fall into the trap of thinking they need to own a little bit of everything. They open their account and feel like they should buy a handful of random stocks just to look like they're doing something. The result is a messy portfolio that's harder to manage and more likely to underperform. Complexity doesn't equal sophistication. In fact, it often hides the opposite. A single broad index fund is more effective than a hodgepodge of random names that looked good in the moment. The mistake isn't in wanting variety—it's in confusing activity with progress.

And let's not forget the emotional missteps. Some beginners put in money they can't afford to lose, like rent money or an emergency fund. When markets wobble, panic sets in, and they yank it all back out at the worst possible time. Investing should never be built on desperation. If you need the money next month, it doesn't belong in the market. Day one is the time to separate your short-term needs from your long-term goals so you never have to pull out money in a rush.

There's also the temptation to chase hot tips right out of the gate. Maybe a friend whispers about a stock that's "about to explode." Maybe you scroll past someone on social media flaunting their crypto gains. The urge to jump in is powerful, especially when you're new and hungry for quick wins. But hot tips are usually just traps dressed up as opportunities. The better move is to keep your focus narrow: start with the boring, proven tools like index funds. Once you're solidly in the game, the noise gets easier to ignore.

The point of dodging these mistakes isn't to avoid every bump in the road—it's to keep small errors from snowballing into disasters. Everyone trips up in the beginning. What matters is that you set yourself up so those trips don't derail your progress. By choosing the right account, avoiding margin, slowing down before clicking, resisting the urge to overcomplicate, and only investing what you can truly spare, you create a smoother path forward.

So on day one, the biggest win isn't picking the perfect stock or timing the perfect trade. It's simply avoiding the landmines that have tripped up countless beginners before you. Get the basics right, keep things simple, and you'll already be ahead of the crowd that rushed in unprepared. Mistakes don't have to define your start—they can be the stories you laugh about later while watching your money quietly grow.

Taxes Without Tears

The word "taxes" sends shivers down spines faster than any stock market crash headline. It conjures images of confusing forms, endless receipts, and the IRS breathing down your neck. But here's the truth: investing taxes don't have to be terrifying. In fact, once you understand the basics, they become just another part of the process—one you can manage without needing to hire an accountant in a three-piece suit. The goal isn't to master tax law; it's to know enough so you can keep more of your money and avoid mistakes that create headaches later.

The first thing to know is that Uncle Sam always wants a piece of the pie. When your investments grow, the government will eventually come knocking. But not all growth is taxed the same way. If you sell an investment for more than you bought it, that's called a capital gain. Hold it for less than a year, and the gain is taxed like ordinary income—often at a higher rate. Hold it for more than a year, and you qualify for long-term capital gains, which are taxed at a lower rate. Translation: patience literally pays. Every extra month you hold on gives you a better deal when it's finally time to cash out.

Now, here's where retirement accounts like IRAs and 401(k)s earn their superhero capes. When you put money into a traditional IRA or 401(k), you often get a tax break right away. That money grows tax-deferred, which means you don't pay taxes on it until you take it out in retirement—when, ideally, you're in a lower tax bracket. Roth accounts flip the script: you pay taxes upfront, but all future growth and withdrawals are tax-free. Either way, these accounts are designed to give you an edge, letting you build wealth faster by keeping the taxman at bay while your money compounds.

If you're investing in a regular brokerage account, the rules are a little different. You'll pay taxes on dividends, which are the payments companies sometimes make to shareholders, and on any capital gains if you sell for a profit. That doesn't mean you should avoid taxable accounts. It just means you should be strategic. For example, if you can hold investments for the long term instead of constantly buying and selling, you'll benefit from those lower long-term capital gains rates. Simplicity is your friend here. The fewer trades you make, the fewer tax events you trigger, and the less paperwork you face come April.

There's also the concept of tax-loss harvesting, which sounds like a farm chore but is actually a way to soften the blow of a bad investment. If one of your investments loses money, you can sell it, lock in the loss, and use it to offset gains elsewhere. It's not about gaming the system—it's about using the rules to your advantage. Even the IRS knows investments don't all win, so they allow you to balance your wins with your losses.

For most beginners, though, the simplest approach is the best: contribute to tax-advantaged accounts first, keep your taxable investments long-term, and don't stress over every possible deduction. You don't need to know the ins and outs of every tax loophole to succeed. You just need a rule of thumb you can actually remember: retirement accounts save you money on taxes now or later, and holding investments longer means less tax pain. That's the one-sentence summary that can guide your decisions without sending you into a spreadsheet spiral.

The emotional relief comes when you realize taxes aren't a monster waiting to ambush you. They're predictable, manageable, and often avoidable if you set up your accounts wisely from the start. The fear is rooted in confusion, and confusion fades when you understand that the system isn't out to punish you for investing—it actually rewards you for being patient and consistent. Once you see taxes as just another factor to plan for, they lose their power to intimidate.

So when April rolls around, don't panic. Know that you've already set yourself up to avoid the worst surprises. Your investments are growing, the tax breaks are working in your favor, and the stress that used to paralyze you has been replaced by calm understanding. Taxes aren't the enemy of investing—they're simply part of the deal. And when you play the game with clarity, you'll find that even the IRS can't take away the peace of knowing you're building wealth the smart way.

Scams, Hype, and the Snake-Oil Parade

Every family has that cousin who swears he's found the next crypto goldmine. You know the type. He talks fast, waves his phone around with screenshots of skyrocketing charts, and makes you feel like you're missing the deal of a lifetime. The truth? Most of those promises belong in the same category as miracle weight-loss pills and late-night infomercials. This is the world of financial scams and hype, and it's been around far longer than TikTok. The names and platforms change, but the game stays the same: exploit confusion, prey on greed, and walk away with your money.

The heart of the problem is that scams don't always look like scams. They show up dressed as opportunity. Multi-level marketing schemes promise financial freedom if you recruit your friends. Penny stock hustlers claim you're about to catch the next Amazon for pennies. Social media gurus post flashy lifestyles and claim their secret trading system will make you rich if you just buy their course. These aren't accidents—they're carefully engineered traps. And they work because they sound convincing, especially when everyone around you seems excited.

One way to disarm these traps is to understand how they appeal to emotion. Scams don't sell investments; they sell dreams. They tell you what you want to hear: that you're smarter than the crowd, that you've found the shortcut, that wealth is just one bold move away. The emotional pull is strong because it dangles certainty in a world where real investing is slow and uncertain. But ask yourself this: if the shortcut really worked, why would they need to sell it to strangers online? The answer, of course, is that you are the product.

History is littered with cautionary tales. Think of Bernie Madoff, who ran one of the largest Ponzi schemes in history. Thousands of people thought they were in on a brilliant strategy, only to learn their wealth had been siphoned away. More recently, the collapse of FTX left countless investors stunned, realizing they had trusted slick branding and celebrity endorsements instead of clear numbers. These stories aren't ancient history—they're reminders that scams thrive in confusion. The more complex or secretive something sounds, the more likely it's designed to deceive.

The role of hype is just as dangerous as outright fraud. Financial media loves to amplify drama. A stock doubles overnight, and suddenly it's the story of the week. A crypto token surges, and influencers scream that you'll regret missing out. Hype feeds on fear of missing out, pushing people to act before they think. But hype is like sugar—it gives a rush, then leaves a crash. By the time most people jump in, the insiders are already cashing out. The losers are always the ones who believed the noise instead of the math.

The relief comes when you realize scams and hype aren't mysteries you can't crack. They follow patterns. If someone promises guaranteed returns, that's a red flag. If you're pressured to invest quickly, that's another. If the pitch depends on secrecy or "exclusive access," it's almost certainly a trap. Real investments don't need hype. They don't require you to pressure friends, dance on social media, or wire money to someone you've never met. Real investments are boring, transparent, and backed by businesses that produce actual goods and services.

This chapter is about arming you with that awareness. Once you learn to see the tricks for what they are, the fear and confusion start to fade. You stop wondering if you're missing the next big thing, and you start recognizing that most "next big things" are just old cons in new clothes. Instead of being dazzled by the parade of snake oil, you can laugh at it and walk on by.

The biggest win here is peace of mind. Scams thrive on urgency and anxiety. But when you're grounded in simple, proven strategies—like the ones you've already learned—you don't need to chase shiny objects. You don't need to keep up with every trend. You can watch the hype machine churn and know, calmly, that your money is safe from it. That's the real freedom: not just building wealth, but building immunity to the noise that tries to steal it from you.

The Red Flags Hall of Fame

If you've ever felt embarrassed for falling for a sketchy ad or a pushy pitch, don't. The history of money is really just the history of people trying to separate you from yours. The only thing that changes are the costumes. Once it was snake oil salesmen rolling into town with potions. Now it's influencers peddling "can't-miss" crypto plays while filming in a rented Lamborghini. The heart of it hasn't changed: hype, manipulation, and the promise of easy money. The difference is that now you get a front-row seat to the Red Flags Hall of Fame.

Multi-level marketing outfits deserve a plaque at the entrance. You've seen them—those companies where you're "selling" a product, but the real money comes from recruiting friends and family. They dress it up with glossy brochures, empowerment slogans, and big promises about financial freedom. But if your income depends more on signing people up than selling something useful, you're not investing—you're participating in a pyramid, one that eventually collapses, leaving most people broke and embarrassed.

Then come penny stocks. These are tiny, obscure companies with shares that trade for pocket change. The pitch is always the same: get in early and you'll be sitting on the next Apple. But here's what really happens. Insiders buy shares, pump up the stock with breathless promises, and then dump them once gullible investors pile in. It's called a pump-and-dump, and it's not new. It's just greed in a trench coat, whispering that you're about to hit the jackpot if you hurry. What most people hit is disappointment.

Social media gurus deserve their own wing. They flood your feeds with flashy cars, exotic vacations, and motivational mantras. They insist that if you just buy their course, subscribe to their signals, or follow their "exclusive" trading method, you'll unlock the secret to wealth. The only secret they're keeping is that their wealth comes from selling the dream, not living it. If you need to film a TikTok dance to pitch your financial plan, odds are the plan is trash.

And let's not forget the wild west of crypto hype. While blockchain technology has real uses, the industry is littered with disasters. Coins with no substance appear overnight, get hyped to the moon, and vanish just as fast. The infamous collapse of FTX isn't some distant, abstract event—it's a flashing neon reminder of how easy it is for slick branding and celebrity endorsements to hide fraud. If something in crypto sounds too good to be true, it probably is. The survivors of these implosions rarely brag online about losing their life savings; all you see are the staged victory laps of those cashing out early.

Every scam and hype cycle relies on urgency. They tell you time is running out, the deal won't last, or everyone else is getting in before you. That's the first red flag. The second is secrecy—if you're told you're one of the lucky few who have access, it's not opportunity, it's manipulation. The third is the promise of guaranteed returns. Real investments don't guarantee anything. They grow because businesses grow, not because someone promised you a magic formula.

The antidote to all this isn't cynicism—it's awareness. Once you know what the red flags look like, they stop being seductive and start looking ridiculous. The cousin pitching a crypto token at Thanksgiving? You'll see him as a walking billboard for desperation, not opportunity. The MLM friend sliding into your DMs about "ground-floor business opportunities"? You'll recognize it for what it is: a dressed-up pyramid scheme that needs you more than you need it. Awareness gives you distance, and distance gives you safety.

The Red Flags Hall of Fame is long and constantly growing. But you don't have to memorize every con. You only need to remember the patterns: urgency, secrecy, guarantees. Those are your tripwires. When you spot them, you don't need to argue, you don't need to prove anyone wrong—you just step aside and let the parade march on without you. That's how you protect your wallet and your peace of mind, and that's how you make sure your money builds wealth instead of fueling someone else's scam.

How to Sniff Out BS in 30 Seconds

Most scams don't announce themselves with a flashing sign. They sneak in dressed as opportunity, hiding behind smooth talk and slick presentation. But the truth is you don't need a finance degree to sniff out bad deals—you just need a mental checklist. The beauty of this checklist is that it works fast. In less than a minute, you can size up an offer, see through the polish, and decide whether it belongs in the trash. Think of it as your personal scam radar, tuned to pick up the signals that scammers can't help but give off.

The first test is the promise test. If someone guarantees you high returns with little or no risk, you're staring at BS. Real investing has ups and downs. There are no promises, no shortcuts, no crystal balls. Anyone who tells you otherwise is selling fantasy, not finance. A steady return of 20% every year? Impossible. A guarantee of never losing money? Impossible. The markets don't work that way, and anyone who says they do is trying to lure you in with lies.

The second test is the urgency test. Scams thrive on pressure. You'll hear lines like, "This deal won't last," or "Only the first ten people get in." The goal is to shut down your ability to think. They don't want you asking questions, because questions kill scams. Real investments don't vanish if you take a week—or a month—to think about them. If someone demands you act immediately, you can bet they don't want you to pause long enough to realize it's garbage.

The third test is the complexity test. Scammers love to drown you in jargon. They'll throw around technical terms, charts, and buzzwords until you're nodding along, too embarrassed to admit you're lost. That's the hook. If you don't understand how something makes money, you shouldn't invest in it. It doesn't matter how sophisticated it sounds. Simplicity is the friend of honest investing. Complexity is the cloak of cons.

The fourth test is the secrecy test. If you're told not to share the opportunity, if it's "exclusive" or "just for insiders," walk away. Scams thrive in shadows. Real investments aren't afraid of sunlight. They're transparent, regulated, and openly discussed. If you can't explain the opportunity to a friend without breaking some imaginary code of silence, it's not an opportunity—it's a trap.

The fifth test is the track record test. Scammers lean on vague testimonials, staged photos, or cherry-picked results. They'll show you someone's supposed million-dollar win but won't show you the thousands of losses behind it. If an investment can't point to a long, verifiable track record with real numbers, it's smoke and mirrors. Legitimate opportunities are boring in their transparency. They show you data, not dreams.

Put all of these together, and you've got a 30-second filter that cuts through the noise. Promises, urgency, complexity, secrecy, and flimsy track records—if you spot any of them, you don't need to argue or investigate further. You can confidently say, "No thanks," and keep your money safe. The power isn't in memorizing every scam out there; it's in recognizing the patterns they all share.

The emotional payoff here is huge. Instead of feeling like prey, you start feeling like the predator—calm, sharp, and unbothered by flashy bait. When your cousin's buddy corners you at a barbecue with the "next big thing," you won't sweat. You'll listen politely, run the checklist in your head, and walk away knowing you saved yourself stress, money, and embarrassment. That confidence builds on itself. With every BS pitch you dodge, you prove to yourself that you're not gullible, you're in control. And that control is what turns fear into freedom.

The 'If It's on TikTok...' Rule

There's a new oracle of financial wisdom in town, and it's not Warren Buffett. It's a teenager with a ring light, shouting about the next big stock in a twelve-second dance clip. Welcome to the modern hype machine, where advice is condensed into viral soundbites and dressed up with flashy editing. The platforms may change, but the danger doesn't: if your financial future fits neatly into a TikTok, it's probably garbage.

The rule here is simple. Viral investing advice is designed for entertainment, not education. The creators want likes, shares, and followers—not necessarily your financial wellbeing. Their incentives are completely misaligned with your goals. A viral post thrives on drama, urgency, and outrageous claims, because that's what spreads. Boring truths like "buy low-cost index funds and hold them for decades" don't exactly light up the algorithm. But they're the truths that actually work.

What makes TikTok-style advice so seductive is its simplicity. Someone says, "This coin is going to 100x," or "Buy this stock before it explodes." The confidence is intoxicating. They speak as if they have insider knowledge, as if they've cracked a code you'd be a fool to ignore. But the reality is they're playing the oldest game in the book: pump up interest, bask in attention, and often sell out while the hype train is still boarding. You're left holding the bag when reality crashes in.

There's no shortage of real-world casualties. Viral videos have sparked frenzies around meme stocks, leaving everyday people pouring in at the peak, only to watch their savings evaporate when the bubble burst. Crypto tokens have surged on the back of TikTok hype, only to collapse days later. The videos that made people rich get shared endlessly. The ones where people lose everything? Those never trend.

The danger isn't just losing money—it's losing judgment. When you're bombarded with flashy clips, your brain starts equating virality with credibility. The repetition makes nonsense sound like truth. And because the content is fast and fun, you don't stop to question it. That's exactly how hype works: slip past your critical thinking while your guard is down.

The antidote is to slow down. If a tip fits neatly into a TikTok, treat it like fast food. Maybe entertaining in the moment, but not the foundation of a healthy diet. Real investing knowledge takes more than a few seconds to explain. It involves context, trade-offs, and long-term thinking. If someone can't explain their strategy in depth, and if you can't find a record of their claims backed by actual numbers, it's not advice—it's performance.

That doesn't mean you should ignore financial content altogether. Social media can be a useful entry point to spark curiosity. But curiosity isn't commitment. When you see a tip, your reflex should be to ask: where's the evidence? Has this strategy worked over decades, or is it just riding a wave of attention today? The more outrageous the promise, the more skeptical you should be.

The emotional payoff comes when you free yourself from the pressure of keeping up with every viral "opportunity." You stop feeling like you're missing out and start recognizing that most of what trends online is just noise. Instead of chasing hype, you stick with boring, proven methods that don't need a hashtag to work. That shift gives you calm, clarity, and protection from the chaos of financial social media.

So here's the golden filter: if the advice is short enough to squeeze into a dance clip, it's not real advice. It's bait. And when you learn to laugh at it instead of fear missing out, you've built the kind of immunity that keeps your money safe in a world obsessed with the next viral moment.

Emails That Want Your Soul

Scams aren't always flashy or viral. Sometimes they slip quietly into your inbox, wearing the disguise of a legitimate message. You open your email and there it is: a subject line promising an urgent opportunity, a warning about account security, or even a chance to get rich quick. These messages are designed to do one thing—trick you into clicking. And once you click, they're after your money, your information, or both.

The first thing to understand is that scam emails are professional-grade manipulations. Gone are the days of broken English and cartoonish promises from foreign princes. Modern phishing emails are slick, branded to look almost identical to the companies they're impersonating. They use real logos, convincing layouts, and urgent language. You'll see subject lines like "Unusual activity detected on your account" or "Claim your exclusive reward before it expires." The goal is always the same: bypass your common sense by triggering fear or excitement.

These emails prey on our instincts. Fear pushes you to click when you think your account has been hacked. Greed pushes you to click when you think you've won a prize. Either way, the scammer wins if you take the bait. The trick is to pause and look closer. Real companies won't demand sensitive information over email. They won't ask for your Social Security number, your passwords, or your credit card details through a link. If an email pressures you into urgency or secrecy, that's your cue to hit delete.

Some scams are more direct. You get a message from a "financial advisor" offering you an inside track on a hot investment. The language is flattering—they'll tell you you're one of the few smart enough to recognize the opportunity. Or you'll see emails with subject lines screaming "Earn passive income NOW" or "This investment will double in weeks." These aren't opportunities. They're hooks. Click through, and you'll find yourself funneled into a pitch for some sketchy scheme or asked to wire money to someone you've never met.

The simplest defense is skepticism. Treat every unsolicited email about money like it's radioactive until proven otherwise. Don't click on links or download attachments unless you're absolutely certain of the sender. Even better, don't engage at all. If something claims to be from your bank or brokerage, log in directly through their official site instead of trusting the link in the message. It takes a few extra seconds, but those seconds can save you from losing thousands.

For scam calls, the same rules apply. The voice on the line may sound authoritative, even threatening, but you hold the power. You don't have to argue or explain yourself. A simple script shuts it down: "Please remove me from your list." Say it calmly, hang up, and don't look back. You don't owe scammers your time, and you don't owe them politeness. The goal is to end the interaction before it hooks you emotionally.

The real power comes when you shift from fear to control. Instead of dreading scam emails and calls, you recognize them as background noise. They lose their sting once you know the red flags. That Nigerian prince has evolved into a fake Amazon security alert, but the principle hasn't changed. They want you rattled enough to act without thinking. Your calm skepticism is the antidote.

The relief comes when you realize you don't need to outsmart every scammer—you just need to avoid stepping into their game. Delete the email. Hang up the phone. Move on. Real opportunities and real companies will never pressure you into rushing, sharing secrets, or sending money to strangers. Once you internalize that, your inbox stops feeling like a minefield and becomes what it was meant to be: a tool you control, not a trap waiting to catch you.

The Anti-FOMO Mindset

If scams prey on greed and fear, hype preys on something even trickier: FOMO, the fear of missing out. This is the feeling that gnaws at you when you hear everyone else is cashing in on the "next big thing." It's the voice in your head whispering that if you don't act now, you'll regret it forever. FOMO is powerful because it's emotional, not logical. It doesn't care about facts or track records. It just wants you to jump before you think. But once you understand how it works, you can train yourself to see through it, step back, and breathe before making a mistake.

The first thing to know about FOMO is that it never shows up at the start of an opportunity. It shows up when something is already peaking. By the time you've heard about the hot stock or crypto coin from your neighbor or on a trending TikTok, the insiders have already made their move. FOMO tricks you into buying high, not investing smart. The stories you hear are carefully curated—the friend who doubled their money brags about it, while the friend who lost half their savings keeps quiet. That silence creates an illusion that everyone is winning but you.

FOMO also feeds on comparison. You scroll through social media and see strangers flashing screenshots of massive gains. You hear co-workers talk about quick wins on the side. It sparks envy, and envy pushes you into rash decisions. The problem is that none of this context is real. You don't see the whole picture. You don't see the losses, the debts, or the risks people took to chase those wins. FOMO sells the highlight reel, never the behind-the-scenes.

The antidote to FOMO isn't just willpower—it's structure. You need to build a system that makes hype irrelevant. When you set up automatic investing into boring, reliable index funds, you no longer feel pressure to chase shiny objects. Your money is already working quietly in the background, compounding day after day. You don't have to make constant choices, so you don't leave room for impulse. That automation is armor. It shields you from your own urges by locking your plan in place.

Another powerful tool is reframing. Instead of seeing a missed opportunity as a loss, see it as protection. Every time you pass on a hyped-up scheme, you've actually saved yourself from the crash that usually follows. That shift turns skipping out on the craze into a win. You're not behind—you're ahead, because you're keeping your money safe while others are lighting theirs on fire.

You can also create rituals to ground yourself during moments of hype. When headlines scream about soaring markets or viral investments, pause and remind yourself of the truth: markets rise and fall, but wealth is built through consistency, not gambling. A simple line you can tell yourself is, "I don't need to win today—I just need to keep building." That phrase acts like a circuit breaker, stopping the surge of panic or envy before it controls your decisions.

The emotional reward of beating FOMO is calm. Instead of feeling like you're constantly one step behind, you start to feel unshakable. You recognize that most people chasing trends aren't building wealth—they're chasing feelings. You don't need to play that game, because you've already chosen a different one. Your game is slow, steady growth. It's the one where patience wins more than genius. And the beauty is that once you see the cycle of hype clearly, you can't unsee it. The urgency that used to pull you in now looks desperate and transparent.

The Anti-FOMO mindset doesn't mean you'll never feel tempted again. It means temptation no longer controls you. You'll still hear the whispers of missed chances, but they'll fade faster each time. What stays is the steady confidence of knowing your money is safe from the rollercoaster of hype. And that confidence is the real payoff—freedom from the noise, focus on your future, and the peace of never letting fear of missing out become the reason you lose out.

The Magic of Long-Term Compounding

What if I told you a single $100 bill could eventually turn into a car, then a house, then the kind of retirement where you wake up when you want instead of when an alarm tells you? Not because you found some secret stock, not because you gambled in crypto, but because you understood compounding. Compounding is the most powerful—and most underrated—force in investing. It doesn't look flashy at first, but over time it transforms small, consistent contributions into life-changing sums. The beauty of compounding isn't just in the math. It's in the relief of knowing you don't have to be a genius, you just have to let time do the heavy lifting.

Here's the simple truth: compounding is growth on growth. Your money earns returns, and then those returns start earning their own returns. Imagine tossing a snowball down a hill. At first it's small, unimpressive, something you could hold in one hand. But as it rolls, it gathers more snow, gets bigger, and accelerates. By the time it reaches the bottom, it's massive. That's what happens with your money when you leave it invested long enough. The snowball doesn't need you to push anymore—it grows because it's rolling.

The tricky part is that in the beginning, compounding feels like nothing. You invest a hundred dollars, and after a year maybe it's $107. Big deal, right? But fast forward twenty years, and that hundred is several hundred, not because you added more but because growth piled on top of growth. Add regular contributions, even tiny ones, and the numbers explode. What looks like a flat line in the early years eventually curves upward, turning into a steep climb. It's the closest thing finance has to magic, except it's entirely predictable and backed by math instead of illusions.

The patience this requires goes against our instincts. Humans crave quick wins and instant gratification. Waiting decades for results feels unnatural. That's why compounding feels boring in the short term. It doesn't deliver adrenaline; it delivers security. But here's the emotional reward: once you truly understand compounding, you stop chasing quick hits. You realize you don't need to gamble or hustle to get ahead. You just need to set your money in motion and keep it there. The stress of trying to "beat the market" melts away when you see that time itself is your ally.

History backs this up. Investors who stayed the course through crashes, recessions, and panics almost always come out ahead. The short-term chaos of markets—the dips, spikes, and headlines—fades into background noise when you zoom out. What remains is the steady upward slope of long-term growth. Compounding doesn't care about the drama of any single year. It rewards consistency, not cleverness. That's why some of the wealthiest people in history, from Warren Buffett to ordinary retirees, all say the same thing: the earlier you start, the bigger the snowball gets.

The emotional hook here is empowerment. You don't need a secret trick. You don't need a golden ticket. You just need to begin. Compounding rewards those who start, not those who wait. Every year you delay, the snowball loses momentum. But every year you invest, even a little, you build speed. And unlike gambling, this isn't a bet—it's a system as reliable as gravity. The only variable is whether you give it enough time to work.

Compounding is where the fear of investing finally flips into excitement. Instead of worrying about losing everything, you begin to imagine what steady, long-term growth can mean for your future. The moment you see how a small contribution can multiply, you get that aha feeling: this is how ordinary people quietly build extraordinary wealth. No lottery tickets, no lucky breaks, no hype—just the quiet, relentless magic of time and consistency.

The $100 Story

Let's put some flesh on the bones of compounding by following a single $100 bill through time. At first glance, $100 doesn't seem like much. It's dinner for two at a decent restaurant, a tank and a half of gas, or a grocery run that somehow still leaves you out of snacks. Most people spend it without thinking. But place that same $100 in the market, let it sit, and suddenly you're not just holding a bill—you're holding a seed with the power to grow into something far larger than its original size.

Here's how it unfolds. Imagine you invest that $100 in a low-cost index fund earning an average annual return of 7%. After one year, your hundred becomes $107. Nothing to celebrate, right? That's just a latte or two. But here's the magic: the following year, you're not just earning on the original hundred—you're earning on the $107. That little bit of extra snow on the snowball now starts pulling its own weight. Year after year, that cycle repeats. By year ten, your hundred is almost $200 without you lifting a finger. By year twenty, it's close to $400. And if you leave it alone for forty years, that forgotten $100 grows into about $1,500. The point isn't the exact math; it's the exponential curve. What felt like pennies at the start snowballs into real power over time.

Now imagine you don't just invest $100 once, but make it a habit. Drop in $100 every month, and the story changes completely. Over forty years, those regular deposits grow into nearly a quarter of a million dollars, assuming that same 7% return. That's the power of compounding married to consistency. You didn't have to guess the next hot stock. You didn't need perfect timing. You simply showed up, month after month, and let the system run.

This is where the emotional punch hits. People often underestimate what small amounts can do because they're thinking in short-term snapshots. A hundred bucks won't change your life today. But stretch the lens out over decades, and that same hundred becomes proof that patience and consistency beat brilliance and luck. It shifts the way you see money. Instead of thinking, "It's just a hundred, it doesn't matter," you start to realize, "Every hundred counts, because every hundred has the potential to multiply."

What makes the $100 story so powerful is that it's accessible. Almost everyone can find a way to scrape together that amount, even if it means cutting back on takeout or skipping a couple of impulse buys. It levels the playing field. Investing isn't just for the wealthy. It's for anyone willing to start, no matter how small. And the earlier you start, the more those small amounts have time to grow.

The kicker is how the math feels compared to how it looks. In the early years, progress feels glacial. Watching your account creep from $100 to $107 isn't thrilling. But stay with it, and the growth curve eventually bends upward in a way that feels unreal. That's the "hockey stick" effect of compounding—the slow grind followed by the sudden surge. The people who build real wealth are the ones who stick around long enough to see that curve bend in their favor.

So the $100 story isn't really about the hundred dollars. It's about the mindset it creates. It proves that money doesn't have to be massive to matter. It proves that time is more powerful than timing. And it proves that the sooner you plant your seed, the bigger the tree will be when you need its shade. That's the lesson: small beginnings, patiently left alone, become extraordinary endings.

Time Is the Superpower

If money is the seed, time is the soil it needs to grow. The greatest mistake new investors make isn't choosing the wrong stock—it's underestimating the power of time. We live in a world that celebrates speed: fast food, overnight shipping, instant downloads. Patience feels outdated. But when it comes to building wealth, time isn't just important—it's the whole game. The earlier you start, the more time you give your money to multiply, and the difference can be staggering.

Picture two people. One begins investing at twenty-five, putting away a modest $200 a month. Another waits until thirty-five to start, but doubles the amount to $400 a month to make up for lost time. They both earn the same return, but by retirement, the early starter ends up with more money—even though they invested less in total. Why? Because those extra ten years gave compounding a head start. Time is like a multiplier that no other strategy can replicate. You can't brute-force it later. Once the years are gone, they're gone.

The emotional weight of this truth is heavy. Many people delay investing because they think they need more money to make it worthwhile. They tell themselves they'll start when they get a raise, or after debts are paid, or once life feels less chaotic. But waiting is the most expensive decision of all. The irony is that the smaller your contributions, the more you need time to do the work for you. Starting early with little beats starting late with a lot almost every time.

It's not about chasing perfection. Nobody starts investing at the perfect age with the perfect plan. What matters is getting in the game as soon as you can, even if it feels insignificant. A $50 contribution at twenty is worth more than $500 at forty, simply because the first dollar has decades to roll downhill like that snowball. Time doesn't just add to your money—it multiplies it in ways that feel invisible at first but undeniable in the long run.

Think of planting a tree. In the early years, it looks like nothing is happening. A fragile sapling barely taller than your knees doesn't look like much of an asset. But give it time, and it grows into something massive, throwing shade, producing fruit, even becoming part of the landscape. That tree is valuable not because you did anything fancy, but because you gave it time. Investing works the same way. You don't need to micromanage or constantly interfere. You just need to let time do its job.

The temptation to shortcut time with clever tricks will always be there. You'll see stories of day traders turning quick profits and wonder if you're missing out. But what they don't show is the burnout, the stress, and the fact that most of those gains don't last. Time doesn't require luck or brilliance. It rewards patience and persistence. The people who win are the ones who stay calm during storms, who trust that the slow, steady process works even when it doesn't feel exciting.

The deeper truth is that time is democratic. It doesn't care about your income, background, or education. Whether you're a high earner with money to spare or someone scraping together small contributions, time gives you the same leverage. The earlier you use it, the more it gives back. That's why the best investment decision isn't picking the right stock—it's starting today instead of tomorrow.

Once you internalize this, investing shifts from being a chore to being a privilege. You start to see every contribution not as a sacrifice, but as buying more time for your money to grow. That mindset is freeing. It removes the pressure to predict the future or beat the market. You don't need to outsmart anyone—you just need to outlast them. And that's the superpower time gives you: the ability to let patience turn small beginnings into extraordinary endings.

Charts That Don't Lie

Numbers on their own feel abstract, but charts have a way of smacking you with reality. They don't just tell you compounding works—they show you. A flat line suddenly curves upward, and in that curve lies the difference between struggling and thriving. When you see the visual story of money left to grow, the logic clicks in a way words can't always capture. It stops being theory and starts being undeniable truth.

Imagine two lines on a chart. One represents someone who starts investing at twenty-five with small monthly contributions. At first, the line creeps upward, barely noticeable. The other line belongs to someone who waits until thirty-five but contributes twice as much. For years, the late starter looks like they're catching up. But then, around midlife, the early line starts to bend upward more sharply. By retirement, the early starter's curve soars far higher, even though they put in less money overall. That's the story of time and compounding told in one simple picture: the early start wins, not because of brilliance, but because of patience.

Charts also reveal the rhythm of the market. When you zoom in on a short period—weeks, months, even a year—the line looks jagged, full of drops and spikes. It feels chaotic, unpredictable, even scary. But zoom out to decades, and the noise fades. The jagged edges smooth into a clear upward slope. Crashes like 2008 or the pandemic downturn of 2020 look terrifying in the moment, but on a long chart they're just dips in an otherwise rising mountain. The message is clear: short-term volatility is drama, but long-term investing is growth.

One of the most powerful visuals is the comparison of starting ages. Place side by side two investors: one who begins at twenty-five and stops at thirty-five, never adding another dollar, and one who waits until thirty-five and invests steadily until retirement. You'd expect the second to come out ahead, right?

But the chart shows the opposite. The early bird's money, left untouched, often ends up larger because compounding had an extra decade to do its work. It's counterintuitive until you see it drawn out—and then it becomes obvious why time trumps effort.

Charts also cut through hype. A viral stock tip might skyrocket on a daily graph, but stretch the lens to years and you often see a flat line or even a collapse. Conversely, boring index funds don't look exciting day to day, but on a thirty-year chart they rise with the steady climb of the economy. This is why seasoned investors swear by long-term data. A chart doesn't care about headlines or hype; it tells the story of sustained growth versus short-term noise.

The emotional impact of these visuals can't be overstated. When you see how small contributions grow into large sums over time, it transforms your mindset. Investing stops feeling like a gamble and starts feeling like building a structure brick by brick. The dips no longer scare you, because the chart shows that dips are temporary. The upward curve reassures you that patience pays, even when the ride feels rough in the moment.

So the next time you doubt whether investing is worth it, picture that chart. Picture the flat Kansas plain that slowly rises until it resembles Everest. Picture the jagged short-term lines smoothed out into a long-term climb. Charts don't lie. They don't sell hype. They just reveal the truth: if you stay the course, the numbers bend in your favor, and the mountain of wealth becomes too tall to ignore.

Compounding in Real Life

It's easy to think of compounding as something abstract that happens in financial charts, but you've already seen it play out in everyday life. The principle is simple: small things repeated consistently snowball into something massive. And whether it's money, habits, or even bad decisions, the pattern is the same. Understanding this makes compounding feel less like math homework and more like a force you can actually see shaping your world.

Think about grocery bills. A box of cereal that cost three dollars a decade ago might now be closer to six. That's compounding in action, only working against you instead of for you. Prices rise year after year, and the increases build on each other until what once felt affordable now makes you mutter at the checkout line. Gasoline works the same way. A few cents here and there may not register at first, but over years, those pennies stack into dollars that change the cost of living. Inflation is just negative compounding. It's money slowly slipping away instead of growing.

You can also see compounding in habits. Skip the gym once, and nothing happens. Skip it regularly, and over time your health takes a hit. Or think about streaming subscriptions. Add one service, then another, and before long you're paying hundreds a year for platforms you barely use. That creep doesn't happen overnight. It compounds slowly until one day you're staring at your bank statement wondering how it all added up.

Now flip the script. Compounding is also why small positive choices become life-changing. Set aside a little money each month, and after years it becomes a financial cushion that feels almost magical. Save energy by switching to efficient lightbulbs, and the lower bills quietly stack up until you've kept hundreds in your pocket. Learn a skill for fifteen minutes a day, and in a few years you're not just dabbling—you're proficient. The math of compounding doesn't care whether you apply it to dollars, calories, or knowledge. It rewards consistency, period.

This is why investing makes so much sense once you see it through the lens of daily life. You already accept compounding in the negative, when prices rise or habits deteriorate. The leap is realizing you can harness the same force in the positive by giving your money a chance to grow on itself. It shifts the question from "Why should I bother?" to "Why would I let this opportunity slip?" If compounding is going to work in some direction no matter what, wouldn't you rather it be for you than against you?

Humor makes this easier to grasp. Think of how Netflix password sharing spread like wildfire—one friend gave it to another, who gave it to another, until suddenly your account was the family entertainment center for people you've never met. That growth wasn't linear. It multiplied. It's the same dynamic behind viral memes, rumor chains, or even moldy leftovers spreading in the fridge. What starts small takes on a life of its own. Money invested consistently works the same way. It may not be glamorous to watch, but it multiplies in the background whether you're paying attention or not.

The key realization is that compounding is always happening, whether you choose to use it or not. Ignore it, and you feel it through rising costs, wasted habits, or lost opportunities. Harness it, and you start to see your future self thank you for the choices you made today. Every contribution becomes a brick in a wall that grows taller and stronger without you having to constantly lift new ones. The secret isn't effort—it's patience and consistency.

Once you connect compounding in money to compounding in life, the concept stops being intimidating. You stop seeing it as an abstract graph and start seeing it as a natural force, like gravity. It doesn't care who you are or what you earn—it only cares whether you give it time to do its work. That recognition is liberating. It turns compounding from a dry financial idea into a daily reminder that small, steady actions—whether financial or personal—have the power to create extraordinary outcomes over time.

Why Patience Pays More Than Genius

In the world of investing, genius gets way too much credit. People imagine you need to outthink Wall Street, decode hidden signals, or discover secret stocks to make real money. But history tells a different story. The true winners aren't the ones making brilliant moves every week—they're the ones who stay calm, stay put, and give their money time to grow. Patience, not genius, is what builds wealth.

The problem is that patience feels passive. It doesn't get you applause. Nobody brags about sitting still while the market bounces up and down. Meanwhile, the news celebrates flashy trades and overnight millionaires. That creates the illusion that success comes from cleverness, when in reality most clever moves blow up. The investors who quietly hold index funds and ignore the noise don't make headlines, but they make fortunes.

Take Warren Buffett, the most quoted investor alive. His secret isn't mystical insight. He started young, invested consistently, and stayed invested for decades. He's said many times that his favorite holding period is "forever." That's not genius. That's discipline. He lets businesses grow, reinvests profits, and doesn't panic when markets stumble. His wealth wasn't built by brilliance in one lucky year—it was built by compounding over many steady decades.

The math backs this up. If you invest steadily and leave your money in the market, history shows that you'll ride through crashes and still come out ahead. The U.S. stock market has faced wars, recessions, oil shocks, inflation spikes, political chaos, and global pandemics. And yet, over the long term, it has always trended upward. Patience turns temporary losses into eventual gains. Impatience turns temporary dips into permanent losses, because selling at the wrong time locks in damage that time would have healed.

Think about the opposite: the genius who jumps in and out of trades, trying to time the market. Even professional fund managers, armed with teams of analysts and mountains of data, fail to consistently beat simple index funds. That's not a coincidence. The market isn't predictable in the short term. Trying to outsmart it is like trying to predict coin flips—it looks doable until you realize how quickly luck runs out. The patient investor doesn't waste energy trying. They know the game isn't about winning every moment—it's about staying in long enough to let compounding work its magic.

Patience also pays emotionally. Every time you resist the urge to panic or chase hype, you buy yourself peace of mind. You don't spend nights refreshing your account in fear. You don't gamble on hunches. You trust the process, and that trust frees you from the stress that wrecks so many investors. That mental calm is as valuable as the money itself. Genius investors often burn out, crushed by the pressure of always trying to outthink the market. Patient investors sleep well at night because they know time is doing the heavy lifting.

The beauty of patience is that it's available to everyone. You don't need a finance degree or insider access. You don't even need perfect timing. All you need is the willingness to start and the strength to stay. That makes patience the ultimate equalizer. It turns ordinary people into successful investors while many so-called geniuses self-destruct.

The aha moment here is simple: you don't have to be brilliant to build wealth. You just have to be steady. Every time you resist the urge to jump ship during a downturn, you prove that your patience is worth more than any clever trade. Over time, those choices add up to wealth that looks like genius from the outside. But you'll know the truth: it wasn't genius at all. It was patience, compounding quietly in your corner, turning consistency into freedom.

What If Everything Crashes?

Every beginner has the same nightmare. You finally work up the courage to invest, put your money into the market, and the next morning you wake up to a headline screaming about a crash. Stocks are tanking, people are panicking, and you feel like you just walked into a casino at the exact moment the dealer rigged the table. The fear is real, and it's not unfounded—crashes happen. But here's the truth: they're not the end of the world. In fact, they're a normal part of the cycle, and if you handle them right, they don't just spare you losses—they set you up for bigger gains.

Look back at history. In 2008, the housing market imploded and the financial system nearly collapsed. The news was apocalyptic, and millions of investors panicked. Those who sold locked in their losses. But those who stayed put, or even invested more, saw their wealth rebound as the market recovered in the following years. By 2013, the market had not only bounced back—it had hit new highs. The same thing happened after the dot-com bubble in 2000, after the September 11 attacks in 2001, and after the COVID-19 crash in 2020. The pattern repeats: markets stumble, sometimes violently, but over the long term they always recover.

Why? Because markets represent businesses, and businesses don't vanish overnight. Even during downturns, companies keep making products, providing services, and solving problems. The economy may slow, but human demand doesn't disappear. Over time, innovation, productivity, and growth push the market higher. That's why every past crash looks terrifying when you're in it, but tiny on a long-term chart. They're speed bumps on a highway that still heads uphill.

The hardest part is the psychology. When you see red numbers in your account, your brain screams, "Get out!" That instinct comes from loss aversion, the natural tendency to feel pain from losses more than joy from gains. But acting on that instinct is what turns paper losses into permanent ones. Selling in a panic is like jumping off a rollercoaster mid-ride. It feels like relief in the moment, but it guarantees injury. Staying strapped in, even when your stomach drops, is the only way to enjoy the ride when it levels out.

This doesn't mean crashes are fun. They're gut-wrenching, stressful, and confusing. But the difference between those who lose and those who win isn't avoiding crashes—it's surviving them. That means holding onto investments instead of fleeing, trusting the long-term pattern instead of fixating on the short-term drop. It also means keeping your contributions steady. Ironically, downturns are when your money buys more shares for the same price. That's like buying stocks on sale. When the recovery comes, those cheap purchases become some of your biggest wins.

You can give yourself a tool for moments like these: a simple script to repeat when panic hits. It goes like this: "This is temporary. The market always recovers. My job isn't to predict the future—it's to stay consistent." Saying it out loud helps calm the emotional storm and remind you of the truth history has already proven. Every great investor has their own version of this mantra because they know the real battle isn't against the market—it's against their own fear.

The emotional payoff of surviving crashes is huge. Once you've lived through one, you realize it's not the end. That realization builds resilience. Instead of dreading the next downturn, you start to see it as an opportunity—a chance to buy more at a discount, a chance to watch patience pay off again. Crashes stop being monsters under the bed and start being just another chapter in the story of growth.

So what if everything crashes? Then you stay calm, you stay invested, and you remind yourself that crashes aren't exceptions—they're part of the process. They test your patience, but they also reward it. And when the dust clears, you'll see that what felt like disaster was really just the market handing you a lesson in why long-term investors always win.

Starter Portfolios That Actually Work

Imagine meal-prepping your money. You don't need a Michelin-star recipe or an Instagram-worthy presentation. You just need a few reliable ingredients you can mix and match without burning down the kitchen. That's what a starter portfolio is—simple, filling, and designed to work without hours of tinkering. The point isn't to impress your coworkers at lunch; it's to keep you full and healthy day after day. Investing is the same. You don't need complexity to succeed. You need a setup that fits your life, grows with you, and gives you confidence to stay the course.

The biggest myth about portfolios is that you need a lot of money to build one. That myth stops people before they even start. But portfolios scale. Whether you have fifty dollars a month or five thousand, the principles are identical. You're just choosing proportions, not chasing exotic flavors. What matters isn't the size of your contributions today but the consistency of those contributions over time. Portfolios are recipes—you can cook them for one or for a crowd. The ingredients don't change, only the portions.

A starter portfolio has three goals. First, it should protect you from unnecessary risk. You don't want to throw your entire paycheck into one stock just because someone on YouTube sounded confident. Second, it should give you exposure to growth. Your money should be working, not lounging around like a lazy roommate. Third, it should be simple enough that you actually stick with it. Complexity kills commitment. A portfolio that looks sleek on paper but gives you anxiety every time you check it isn't a good portfolio—it's a stress machine.

So what does this look like in practice? It looks like boring investments with proven track records: index funds, ETFs, and bonds. No guessing which company will dominate the future. No scrambling to keep up with every headline. Just steady exposure to the overall economy, balanced with a cushion for stability. When you spread your money across these building blocks, you're diversifying. That means if one piece stumbles, the others keep you upright. It's the financial version of not putting all your eggs in one basket, except instead of eggs you've got your future.

The brilliance of starter portfolios is that they can be tailored to different lives. If you're broke but determined, there's a plan for that. If you're a middle-income earner trying to build momentum, there's a setup for you too. If you're a high earner sitting on cash but scared of losing it, you can build a portfolio that avoids rookie mistakes. And if you're risk-averse, you can lean on safer allocations without feeling like you're missing out. Each version has its quirks, but all share the same DNA: simple, diversified, and designed for real humans instead of financial robots.

The emotional shift this creates is massive. Instead of staring at the market like a storm you can't control, you start feeling like you've got a sturdy house built on a hill. Crashes and hype no longer dictate your mood. You know your money is organized, working quietly in the background, and growing while you live your life. That peace of mind is the true value of a starter portfolio. It's not just numbers—it's confidence.

The next sections will break down real-world examples of portfolios for different situations. You'll see how even tiny contributions can snowball, how balanced setups create stability, and how cautious plans protect peace of mind. These aren't hypothetical schemes. They're practical recipes you can follow today, adjusted to your income, your risk tolerance, and your goals. The point isn't to impress Wall Street. It's to make your financial life simple, strong, and sustainable.

Starter portfolios aren't about showing off. They're about building something that works without consuming your time or sanity. Once you see how easy it is to set one up, the fear of "not knowing what to do" dissolves. What you're left with is clarity, momentum, and the feeling that you've finally turned investing from a source of anxiety into a quiet engine of freedom.

The Broke-but-Building Plan

There's a myth that investing is only for people with disposable income, the ones sipping lattes while casually tossing hundreds into the market every month. But the truth is, even if you're scraping by, you can still invest. The Broke-but-Building plan is proof that you don't need wealth to begin—you just need consistency and a willingness to start with what you've got. Fifty bucks may not sound like much. It might feel like spare change compared to what the big players move around. But in the world of compounding, fifty bucks can eventually grow into something meaningful. The key is to stop waiting for the "perfect time" and start with the time you already have.

Let's be clear. If you're barely covering rent, utilities, and groceries, investing isn't the first step—stability is. An emergency fund comes before any portfolio. But once you've carved out even a little breathing room, you can begin. The beauty of this plan is that it's designed to make you feel empowered instead of overwhelmed. Fifty dollars is the price of a night out, a delivery binge, or a new pair of shoes. Redirecting that into your future isn't deprivation—it's transformation.

So how does it work? The foundation is an index fund or ETF that tracks the overall stock market. Why? Because it gives you instant diversification without demanding you pick winners and losers. With a single investment, your fifty dollars buys tiny slices of thousands of companies. That means you're not betting on one business—you're betting on the economy as a whole. It's like turning your small contribution into a ticket on the entire growth of human progress. Boring? Absolutely. Effective? Undeniably.

The trick is automation. When money is tight, it's tempting to skip contributions. But by setting up an automatic transfer—even just fifty dollars a month—you remove willpower from the equation. Your future self keeps getting paid, even when your present self feels strapped. And because the amounts are small, you can often make them work by shaving little habits: cutting one streaming service, cooking dinner twice instead of ordering out, or skipping a few impulse buys. These tiny sacrifices compound into something far greater than their immediate value.

The emotional payoff is enormous. When you're broke, money feels like something that happens to you, not something you control. Bills, debts, and unexpected expenses dictate your mood. But the moment you set aside even fifty bucks for investing, the power shifts. You're no longer just surviving—you're building. That mental switch from helplessness to agency is as valuable as the growth itself. It tells you: I may not be rich today, but I'm creating a path toward being richer tomorrow.

Over time, this plan builds confidence. At first, you'll barely notice the growth. A few months in, you might have a couple hundred dollars, which still feels small. But as the years pass, that account starts to swell. You'll look back and realize that the habit mattered more than the size. You didn't need to wait until you had thousands. You needed to start with dozens and let them stack. Each deposit becomes a reminder that your financial story is changing, one month at a time.

The Broke-but-Building plan isn't glamorous. It won't get you bragging rights at parties. But that's the point. Quiet, consistent effort beats loud, reckless bets every time. Starting with fifty dollars proves that investing isn't reserved for people who already have wealth. It's for anyone willing to show up, plant seeds, and give them time to grow. The size of the seed doesn't matter as much as the decision to plant it. And once you've planted, the soil of time and consistency will take care of the rest.

Middle-Income Momentum

If the Broke-but-Building plan is about proving that anyone can start, the Middle-Income Momentum plan is about turning steady cash flow into serious traction. You've got more wiggle room now. The bills are paid, the fridge has food, and you're not sweating every unexpected expense. This is the moment to harness that breathing room and push your money into motion. The difference between staying comfortable and building real wealth lies in what you do with this stage of your income.

At this level, the temptation is lifestyle creep. You get a raise, and suddenly you're eating out more, upgrading gadgets, or buying clothes you don't really need. None of these are bad in moderation, but if all of your extra income gets absorbed by spending, you're stuck in the same cycle as before—working harder without getting ahead. Middle income is where people often get trapped in "comfortable broke." They look fine on the outside but have nothing growing behind the scenes. The antidote is momentum: channeling some of that extra into investments that keep compounding even while you sleep.

Here's the core idea: build a balanced mix of growth and safety. With more income, you can go beyond bare-bones investing and add some structure. A strong middle-income portfolio usually combines broad index funds with a sprinkle of bonds or bond ETFs for stability. The index funds give you growth exposure to thousands of companies, while the bonds act as ballast when the market wobbles. It's not about chasing huge wins—it's about keeping your ship steady while it sails forward.

One of the smartest moves here is increasing contribution size without overthinking it. If you're able to invest a few hundred dollars a month, set that number in stone and automate it. Pretend it's another bill you can't skip. That way, your wealth builds in the background without demanding your constant attention. The mistake many make is tinkering—constantly adjusting contributions, pulling money out for minor expenses, or trying to time the market. Momentum only works if you keep the engine running without interruption.

This stage also allows you to take advantage of tax-advantaged accounts. If your employer offers a 401(k) with matching contributions, grab it—it's free money. If you're eligible for an IRA, contribute there too. Tax benefits might not feel exciting today, but they supercharge compounding by keeping more of your money invested instead of handing it to the government early. A middle-income earner who locks into these vehicles often ends up with dramatically more wealth than someone with higher income who never bothered.

The emotional beat here is empowerment. You've graduated from scraping by to shaping your future. You're not just planting seeds anymore—you're tending a garden. You see your account balances grow, and you start to realize that money isn't just something you earn and spend—it's something you can put to work. That mental shift is addictive in the best way. Once you've tasted momentum, it's hard to go back to letting money sit idle.

This plan also builds resilience. By having a diversified, balanced portfolio, you're less rattled by downturns. You know your bonds provide stability when stocks stumble, and you know your regular contributions buy more during dips. That confidence keeps you invested through rough patches, which is exactly what turns momentum into long-term success.

Middle-Income Momentum isn't about becoming flashy or chasing quick wins. It's about building a system that works in the background, fueled by the consistency you can now afford. Done right, it sets you on a trajectory where every raise, every bonus, and every bit of extra income accelerates your progress instead of vanishing into lifestyle creep. The magic isn't in how much you make—it's in how much you keep moving forward. Momentum compounds just like money, and once you've got it, your financial growth becomes unstoppable.

The High-Earner but Clueless Kit

High income doesn't automatically translate into wealth. Plenty of people making six figures or more end up with little to show for it because they fall into the trap of thinking their paycheck alone is enough. They keep money sitting in checking accounts, dabble in too many funds at once, or chase exotic investments to feel sophisticated. The High-Earner but Clueless Kit exists to strip away that noise and channel big cash flow into simple, effective growth. Because earning a lot doesn't help if the money isn't working for you.

Here's the reality: high earners often have more room to make mistakes. That's a blessing and a curse. A bloated paycheck makes it easier to shrug off bad spending or lazy investing. But over time, wasted opportunities pile up. Sitting on a mountain of cash in a low-interest savings account is just letting inflation eat away at your hard work. And scattering money across seventeen funds with fancy names isn't diversification—it's confusion. What you need isn't complexity. It's clarity.

The kit starts with the same foundation as everyone else: broad index funds. The reason doesn't change just because your salary is bigger. Index funds give you ownership in thousands of companies, spreading your risk while capturing growth. The difference is scale. Instead of adding fifty or a hundred a month, you're feeding these funds with bigger, consistent contributions. That magnifies the compounding effect dramatically. The math works the same way; the zeros just get added faster.

Next is safety. High earners often underestimate the value of stability because they assume they can just "earn more" if something goes wrong. That mindset is dangerous. Part of this kit involves keeping a cushion in safer assets like bonds or bond ETFs, enough to let you sleep at night during downturns. When you've got more money on the line, the swings can feel harsher, even if the percentages are the same. Balance prevents panic.

Another element of this plan is avoiding vanity investing. It's tempting, once you're making real money, to prove your financial savvy by picking stocks, buying into private deals, or diving into complicated strategies. But most of the time, those moves don't outperform the basics. Worse, they create unnecessary stress. The kit cuts through that impulse. Stick to a core portfolio that does the heavy lifting, and if you want to scratch the itch of speculation, carve out a small percentage as "fun money" you can afford to lose. That way, you protect your wealth while indulging your curiosity.

Tax strategy also becomes more important here. High earners face bigger tax bills, which makes it crucial to use every advantage available. Maxing out retirement accounts, contributing to HSAs, or exploring tax-efficient investments can save thousands every year. That's money that stays in your compounding machine instead of leaving your pocket. Getting this right often makes the difference between being rich on paper and actually building sustainable wealth.

The emotional beat of this kit is humility. A fat paycheck can trick you into thinking you've mastered money, but income is temporary. Jobs change, industries shift, and lifestyles expand faster than you realize. Wealth is what you keep, not what you make. This plan forces you to recognize that and put systems in place so your money grows even if your career takes a left turn.

Done right, the High-Earner but Clueless Kit replaces scattered, flashy attempts with a streamlined, powerful approach. It keeps you from sabotaging yourself with complexity and ensures your income turns into lasting wealth. The relief comes when you realize you don't need to juggle endless options to feel in control. You need to focus, automate, and let time multiply your advantage. Earning more is only half the story. Making it grow is what gives you freedom.

The 'I Hate Risk' Setup

Not everyone has the stomach for volatility. Some people break out in a sweat when their account dips by even a few dollars. If the thought of losing money keeps you up at night, your plan doesn't need to mimic the risk appetite of someone who thrives on rollercoasters. The 'I Hate Risk' Setup exists for the cautious investor who values peace of mind as much as returns. The goal isn't to maximize growth at all costs. It's to grow steadily, avoid gut-wrenching swings, and actually stay invested because you're comfortable with the ride.

The first principle here is preservation. You're not chasing the biggest returns—you're protecting the money you've worked hard to earn. That means leaning heavier on safer assets like bonds, bond ETFs, and even high-yield savings or CDs. These options won't make your portfolio soar overnight, but they also won't send you into a panic spiral when the market dips. Think of them as the sturdy bricks in your financial foundation. They may not shine, but they'll hold steady through storms.

That doesn't mean avoiding stocks entirely. Even the most risk-averse investor needs some exposure to growth, or inflation will quietly eat away at your savings. But the balance is tilted. Instead of an aggressive stock-heavy mix, this setup might look closer to half stocks and half bonds, or even more conservative depending on your comfort level. The point is control—you decide the level of risk you can tolerate, and you design your portfolio around it. When you know your downside is limited, you're far less likely to make rash decisions.

The second principle is simplicity. Complicated portfolios create anxiety because they're hard to monitor. A cautious investor doesn't need ten different asset classes to feel secure. Two or three core holdings—a total stock market index fund, a bond fund, and maybe a cash-equivalent account—are more than enough. Clarity reduces stress, and stress reduction is exactly why you chose this path.

What makes this plan powerful isn't just the asset mix—it's the emotional freedom it delivers. When markets stumble, the aggressive investors are busy refreshing apps, wondering if they should sell. You, meanwhile, are calm because your bonds are holding steady and your exposure to stocks is manageable. That calmness is priceless. It keeps you from bailing out during downturns, which is the real danger for risk-averse investors. Fear-driven exits ruin returns far more than conservative allocations ever do.

The 'I Hate Risk' Setup also reframes success. For you, success isn't about bragging rights or hitting the highest possible return. It's about confidence, consistency, and sleep. If you can invest for decades without panic, you'll almost certainly come out ahead of people who swung for the fences but burned out along the way. Wealth isn't just measured in numbers—it's measured in the peace you feel knowing your future is secure.

And here's the deeper truth: avoiding risk doesn't mean avoiding growth. It means defining growth on your own terms. You're not saying no to investing—you're saying yes to investing in a way that matches your temperament. That alignment is the key to longevity. If your portfolio feels like a good fit for your personality, you'll stick with it. And sticking with it, not chasing the maximum possible return, is what actually builds wealth over time.

The emotional beat of this plan is relief. Instead of dreading every headline or market swing, you start to feel steady. You know your money is protected, you know it's growing at a pace you can handle, and you know you won't be derailed by fear. That's what the 'I Hate Risk' Setup delivers—not just financial stability, but the freedom to invest without anxiety.

Sample Allocations in Plain English

Most investing books throw pie charts at you like you're prepping for a corporate meeting. Slices of blue and green, neat percentages, and a legend so tiny you'd need a magnifying glass. That's not what you need. You need something as clear as a recipe card. You want to know what goes where, how much of it, and what it does for you. So here's the truth: a portfolio is nothing more than a plate of financial ingredients. And just like a meal, you want a balance of protein, carbs, and veggies—or in this case, growth, safety, and stability.

Think of the classic balanced portfolio. It's like a hearty dinner: half growth, half stability. In plain English, that's something like half in a total stock market index fund and half in a bond fund. The stock fund is your growth engine, pulling your money forward over decades. The bond fund is your stabilizer, keeping you from panicking when stocks take a dive. Together, they give you nutrition without heartburn.

For someone younger or more comfortable with risk, the plate tilts more toward stocks. Picture seventy percent stocks and thirty percent bonds. That's like loading your meal with extra protein because you've got years to burn it off. The stock-heavy side makes your money work harder, but you've still got a cushion from the bonds to keep you steady during rough patches. Over the long haul, that tilt can mean more growth, but you have to be ready to watch your portfolio bounce around without losing sleep.

For someone who hates risk, the plate tilts the other way. Imagine thirty percent stocks and seventy percent bonds. That's like choosing comfort food—safe, filling, not too spicy. You won't see your money double in dramatic leaps, but you'll have the security of knowing it won't crater when the market throws a tantrum. This setup trades speed for calm, and calm is often what keeps people invested long enough to actually benefit.

Now let's talk about the simplest recipe: one index fund. Yep, just one. A total market index fund or an S&P 500 index fund is like a financial casserole. It's not glamorous, but it feeds you well and covers the bases. With a single fund, you own pieces of hundreds or thousands of companies. That's diversification baked right in. For beginners, this can be the most stress-free option because you don't need to manage multiple moving parts.

For those with a little more appetite, you can split your plate into three items: a total U.S. stock fund, an international stock fund, and a bond fund. This adds variety without chaos. The international slice gives you exposure to companies outside the U.S., which spreads risk further. The bond fund keeps things grounded. The U.S. stock fund powers most of the growth. Together, they form a meal that feels balanced, with just enough spice to keep it interesting.

The beauty of talking in plain English is that you don't get lost in jargon. When someone says "allocation," they really just mean, "What percentage of my money goes where?" And when you think of it like a recipe, it stops being intimidating. You don't need to memorize ratios—you just need to decide what mix makes you feel comfortable. Once you've chosen your recipe, automation does the cooking for you. Every deposit goes into the same mix, month after month, building a steady meal that compounds over time.

The emotional beat here is clarity. Instead of staring at pie charts and pretending to understand them, you walk away knowing exactly what your plate looks like. You see that it's not mysterious or complicated—it's just proportions. And when you understand the recipe, you stop second-guessing yourself. You stop wondering if you're "doing it wrong." You realize that the right portfolio isn't about perfection. It's about choosing the mix that fits your taste and sticking with it long enough to let time and compounding serve the results.

Mini Case Studies: Maria vs. Jake

Stories stick better than formulas, so let's step into the lives of two fictional but familiar characters: Maria and Jake. Their choices reveal the difference between steady investing and hype-chasing, and show how real people can either harness compounding or sabotage themselves with impatience.

Maria is thirty years old and earns a steady income from her job as a nurse. She doesn't have a finance degree, and she doesn't read investment blogs late at night. But five years ago she opened a retirement account and decided on a simple plan: put $300 a month into a total stock market index fund and ignore the noise. She set up automatic deposits so she wouldn't have to think about it. When the market dipped, she didn't panic. When it soared, she didn't tinker. Maria's approach wasn't flashy, but her account grew steadily. After five years, her balance showed tens of thousands of dollars, not because she picked winners but because she stayed the course. Her reward isn't just the money—it's the calm confidence that she's building a future on her own terms.

Jake, on the other hand, works in marketing and makes about the same income. He also wanted to invest, but he got hooked on social media gurus who promised quick riches. He poured his savings into meme stocks, crypto, and whatever was trending that week. For a while, he bragged about his wins at parties. But the rollercoaster of gains and losses left him exhausted. One week he doubled his money; the next, he lost half of it. Over time, his portfolio was worth less than if he had just put money into a boring index fund. Worse, he developed a constant fear of missing out, always convinced the next hot tip would save him. Jake's story shows the cost of impatience: stress, losses, and wasted time.

These two examples highlight the emotional difference as much as the financial one. Maria feels steady. She doesn't check her account every day because she doesn't need to. She trusts the process, and that trust gives her peace. Jake feels anxious. His money is a source of drama instead of security, and every headline feels like a personal crisis. The contrast is sharp: one person builds wealth quietly, the other burns energy chasing illusions.

To complete the picture, let's add Sam. Sam didn't start investing until forty-five. For years, he told himself he was too busy, too broke, or that he'd start later. By the time he finally opened an account, he worried it was too late. But Sam committed to putting away $500 a month into a balanced portfolio of stocks and bonds. Twenty years later, at sixty-five, Sam had built a respectable nest egg. It wasn't as large as Maria's, but it was more than enough to give him security in retirement. Sam's story shows that while starting early is ideal, starting late is still powerful. The real mistake is never starting at all.

Together, these case studies prove the central lesson: steady beats flashy, and patience beats panic. Maria wins not because she's smarter, but because she's consistent. Jake loses not because he's unlucky, but because he let hype drive his decisions. Sam shows that even if you've delayed, there's still hope if you commit. These aren't abstract lessons—they're real paths people walk every day. And once you see them side by side, the choice becomes obvious: follow the boring, proven road of consistency, or gamble on the emotional highs and lows of hype.

The emotional beat is recognition. Readers will see themselves in Maria, Jake, or Sam, and that self-awareness becomes fuel for change. It's not about perfection—it's about choosing the path that aligns with your long-term peace and prosperity. The takeaway is clear: investing isn't a contest of brilliance. It's a contest of behavior. The person who sticks with steady contributions wins almost every time.

Automating Success and Sleeping at Night

Checking your balance every day is like weighing yourself after every cookie. It doesn't tell you anything useful, and it only makes you feel guilty. The smartest investors aren't the ones glued to their accounts; they're the ones who set up systems that run without constant supervision. Automation is the closest thing to a cheat code in investing. It transforms saving and investing from a daily battle of willpower into a background process that works while you live your life. The beauty of this chapter is that once you grasp automation, you'll realize building wealth doesn't have to be dramatic or stressful. It can be boring, and boring is brilliant.

Automation starts with regular contributions. When you set up direct deposits or automatic transfers into your investment account, you remove choice from the equation. You don't debate whether to invest each month—you just do it. That consistency fuels compounding and stops procrastination from derailing you. It's the financial equivalent of setting your alarm to brew coffee every morning. You don't need to think about it, and yet you still get the benefit day after day.

The second layer is automating account allocation. Once your money hits your investment account, you can direct it to flow into the funds you've chosen without lifting a finger. Most brokerages let you select where contributions go, so your balanced portfolio stays balanced without you constantly tinkering. This prevents emotional decisions during market swings and guarantees that your long-term plan keeps humming along. Automation protects you from yourself, and that's a gift most investors underestimate.

Another piece of automation is rebalancing. Over time, your portfolio shifts as stocks rise or bonds dip. Without correction, you might end up more aggressive or more cautious than you intended. Annual rebalancing resets the proportions, but even this can be automated. Some accounts let you schedule it, while others require a quick yearly check-in. Either way, the point is to make maintenance rare and simple. One small adjustment each year is enough to keep your portfolio healthy.

The emotional payoff of automation is peace. Instead of wondering if you're doing enough or worrying you've missed a step, you know the system is running. You don't need to log in constantly, chase hot tips, or stress about every dip. Your energy shifts from reacting to headlines to living your actual life. That's why people who automate not only build more wealth but also report less stress about money. They've shifted the burden from daily decision-making to a set-it-and-forget-it system.

Automation also cures the disease of over-checking. Every time you peek at your account, you invite fear or greed to take the wheel. See red numbers and you panic. See green numbers and you're tempted to add recklessly. Automation removes the need to peek. You already know the process is working, so you can step away. That distance keeps your emotions in check and your patience intact. It's the difference between constantly refreshing a tracking number and just trusting the package will arrive.

The most liberating part of automation is the freedom it gives you to be boring. Boring portfolios don't need daily drama. They don't require constant tweaking. They just work, quietly and efficiently, while your attention is free for everything else in life. That freedom is the true reward of automation. It's not just about money—it's about reclaiming your time and your sanity. With the right systems in place, you can build wealth and sleep at night, confident that the machine you set in motion is carrying you toward financial independence.

Set It, Forget It, Get Rich Anyway

The best-kept secret in investing isn't a hot stock or a hidden trick—it's the ability to set things up once and walk away. Imagine planting a tree, watering it a few times at the start, and then letting rain and sunlight do the rest. That's what automatic investing is: plant the seed, step back, and let nature—compounding, in this case—handle the heavy lifting. The less you fuss with it, the more it grows. The irony is that most people believe they need to constantly monitor, tweak, or optimize. In reality, the people who touch their investments the least usually end up doing the best.

The core of this approach is automation. When you set a fixed amount of money to flow into your account every month, you remove hesitation. You don't get stuck wondering if now is the right time to invest or if you should wait until the market settles. The truth is, the right time is always now. Automating turns investing into a bill you pay yourself first, without question. Just like rent or utilities, it comes out on schedule. You may not notice it at first, but over time, that quiet drip becomes a river.

This system also shields you from your own worst instincts. Left to our own devices, we tend to get emotional about money. A scary headline might make us stop investing. A sudden boom might tempt us to throw in more than we can afford. Automation keeps you steady through both. It doesn't care about your mood, the news cycle, or what your cousin swears is the next big thing. It just does the work, rain or shine, bull market or bear market.

One of the most powerful effects of "set it and forget it" is that it frees your brain. Instead of wasting energy wondering if you're saving enough, you already know the system is in motion. Instead of stressing about timing, you know your money is flowing in at regular intervals. That frees you to focus on your life, not your account balance. The best investors aren't glued to screens—they're busy living, because they know their portfolios are quietly compounding in the background.

Real-life proof of this strategy comes from studies of retirement accounts. People who signed up for automatic contributions and then ignored them often ended up with larger balances than the ones who checked in constantly and made adjustments. Why? Because the steady contributors didn't interrupt the process. They let compounding do its thing, uninterrupted. The constant tinkerers, on the other hand, often pulled money out during dips or skipped contributions when they got nervous. In other words, activity hurt them. In investing, less really is more.

The emotional relief here can't be overstated. There's something incredibly calming about knowing you don't need to micromanage every detail. You're not standing over your investments like a nervous chef watching the oven. You set the timer, walk away, and come back later to see the meal perfectly cooked. That distance keeps you from burning yourself out. It also makes investing sustainable. If something feels like work, you'll eventually quit. If it runs automatically, you'll keep going for decades—and decades are where compounding shines.

The brilliance of this system is its simplicity. Anyone can set it up. You don't need advanced knowledge, complex tools, or constant oversight. You need one decision: how much to invest each month. After that, automation handles the rest. The hardest part is starting. Once it's in place, your future self takes over, building wealth while you carry on with your life. That's why the phrase "set it and forget it" isn't just catchy—it's the closest thing to a guarantee in investing. Forget the drama, forget the tinkering. Just plant the seed, let it grow, and enjoy the peace of knowing the system is working for you every single day.

The Paycheck Split Trick

Most people think of investing as something you do after everything else is paid. Rent, groceries, Netflix, and whatever's left over goes into savings or, if you're disciplined, into an investment account. The problem is that "whatever's left over" usually ends up being nothing. Life always finds a way to eat that extra cash. That's why the Paycheck Split Trick is so powerful. Instead of treating investing as an afterthought, you bake it into the process from the start. The moment your paycheck arrives, part of it gets funneled into your investments automatically. You don't see it, you don't debate it, you don't even miss it—because it's gone before you can spend it.

Here's how it works. Most employers will let you split your direct deposit into multiple accounts. That means you can send, say, eighty percent to your regular checking account and twenty percent straight into your investment account. If you're self-employed or your employer doesn't offer this option, you can set up an automatic transfer on payday. The principle is the same: the money moves before you get the chance to touch it. It's like financial sleight of hand, tricking yourself into saving and investing without relying on willpower.

The beauty of this system is that it makes investing invisible. You don't feel like you're giving something up every month, because you never had the chance to think of that money as spending money. It's like taxes—they come out before you even see your paycheck, so you learn to live without them. The difference is that this "tax" is one you impose on yourself, and instead of going to the government, it goes to your future.

One way to make this stick is to use a script with your HR department. It doesn't need to be complicated. Something like: "Hi, I'd like to set up my direct deposit so that 80% of my paycheck goes to my checking account and 20% goes to this brokerage account. Can you help me fill out the form?" That's it. No financial jargon, no complicated instructions. Just a simple request that locks in a habit you'll benefit from for decades.

If you're nervous about committing too much, start small. Even five or ten percent is enough to build momentum. The key is consistency, not size. Once you've adjusted to living on the slightly smaller paycheck, you can increase the percentage over time. You'll be surprised how quickly your spending adapts. Humans are masters of adjusting to what's in the bank. If less is available, you naturally scale down without even noticing.

The emotional payoff is huge. Instead of constantly worrying if you're saving enough, you know the system is running. Every payday, your future self gets paid before your present self starts spending. That shift rewires the way you see money. You stop thinking of investing as optional and start seeing it as essential. Over time, this creates a quiet confidence that builds with every deposit.

The Paycheck Split Trick turns your income into a wealth machine by removing human error. You don't need to be disciplined every month—you only need to be disciplined once, when you set it up. After that, inertia does the work for you. It's the simplest, smartest way to ensure you're always moving forward, no matter what else is happening in your life.

The Rebalancing Ritual

Think of your portfolio like a closet. Over time, things get out of order. The shirts migrate to one side, the shoes pile up, and suddenly the balance is gone. Investing works the same way. As the market shifts, your original mix of stocks and bonds drifts. Left alone, your portfolio might become riskier than you wanted or too conservative for your goals. That's where the Rebalancing Ritual comes in. Once a year, you pull everything out, tidy it up, and put it back in the right proportions. It's spring cleaning for your money, and it takes far less time than scrubbing out a closet.

Here's why it matters. Imagine you started with 70% stocks and 30% bonds. After a strong year in the stock market, that mix might quietly drift to 80/20. Now you're exposed to more risk than you originally signed up for. A rough patch could hit harder than you expected. Rebalancing brings things back in line. You sell off a bit of what grew too much, buy a little more of what fell behind, and restore the balance. It may feel counterintuitive—selling what's winning and buying what's lagging—but that discipline locks in gains and positions you to benefit when the cycle turns.

The good news is that this isn't a daily or even monthly task. Once a year is usually enough. Pick a date—your birthday, New Year's, tax season, whatever sticks—and make it your annual money ritual. Log into your account, look at your allocation, and nudge it back to your target mix. If your brokerage offers automatic rebalancing, even better. Set it once, and it'll quietly maintain the balance for you.

The ritual isn't just mechanical. It's psychological. It gives you a structured reason to check in on your money without spiraling into overthinking. Instead of logging in every week to chase headlines, you know you have one designated check-up a year. That control keeps you calm the rest of the time. You don't need to react to every market swing because you trust that your annual ritual will handle the drift.

Rebalancing also teaches humility. It reminds you that no single investment wins forever. The parts of your portfolio that lag today might lead tomorrow. By systematically restoring balance, you resist the temptation to chase what's hot. You're not guessing—you're following a plan. That discipline is what separates investors who build steady wealth from those who burn out trying to predict the unpredictable.

Some investors like to turn this into a checklist. Step one: check your allocation. Step two: compare it to your target. Step three: make the adjustments. That's it. The whole thing can take less than an hour once a year. For the rest of the year, you're free to ignore the noise. The ritual gives you a sense of control without constant interference. It's like brushing your teeth—you don't think about it all day, but doing it regularly keeps everything healthy.

The emotional beat here is reassurance. Rebalancing isn't exciting, but it's grounding. It proves you're not drifting blindly. You have a system. You know your money is aligned with your goals. And that knowledge makes it easier to stay invested through ups and downs. The Rebalancing Ritual is small, steady maintenance that pays off with decades of calm growth. You don't need brilliance or constant action—just one annual habit that keeps your financial closet neat and your future on track.

Why Checking Too Often Is a Disease

Imagine stepping on a scale after every sip of water. You'd drive yourself crazy. The fluctuations wouldn't mean anything, but they'd mess with your head all the same. That's what happens when investors check their accounts too often. Every wiggle feels like a crisis. A one-day dip feels like doom, a one-day rise feels like a jackpot, and the constant rollercoaster of emotions leads to bad decisions. Checking too often is a disease, and it spreads fast in a world where your portfolio is just a tap away on your phone.

The problem isn't just wasted time. It's the way constant checking distorts your perception. When you stare at daily or hourly changes, you lose sight of the long-term trend. The market moves like a heartbeat—up and down, up and down—but the overall direction over decades is upward. If you zoom in too close, all you see are the jitters. That narrow focus makes it hard to stay calm. It's like watching waves crash on the shore without noticing the tide is rising.

Every investor who refreshes their account daily thinks they're "staying informed." What they're really doing is marinating in anxiety. Each red number feels like failure, even if it's just normal volatility. That anxiety leads to mistakes: selling when you should hold, chasing when you should wait. The irony is that by trying to stay in control, you actually lose it. Checking often doesn't give you clarity—it clouds your judgment.

Think about how portfolio swings affect your emotions. Say your balance drops by 5% in a week. If you weren't watching, you wouldn't even know. But because you saw it, you feel pain. Loss aversion—the human tendency to hate losing more than we love winning—kicks in. You're tempted to hit the panic button. Now imagine you hadn't checked until the end of the year, and by then, the market had recovered. The dip would be invisible. Same money, different perspective, completely different stress levels.

The solution is to set boundaries. Treat your portfolio like an oven. You don't stand there opening the door every two minutes to check on the cookies—you set the timer and walk away. With investments, your timer might be quarterly or yearly. That's enough to confirm things are on track without letting short-term noise dictate your mood. Automation makes this easier. When you know contributions and allocations are running in the background, there's no reason to peek constantly.

This isn't just about sanity. It's about performance. Studies show that investors who trade more often usually earn less than those who leave their money alone. Why? Because frequent checking leads to frequent fiddling, and fiddling usually means buying high, selling low, and locking in regret. The less you interfere, the more your portfolio compounds without interruption. Inactivity, counterintuitively, is a superpower.

The emotional beat here is freedom. By breaking the habit of over-checking, you free yourself from the seesaw of fear and greed. Your money stops being a daily source of stress and becomes what it should be: a background engine quietly working for you. Instead of reacting to every bump, you live your life knowing the system is solid. You stop treating your portfolio like a clingy ex who needs constant attention, and you start treating it like a long-term partner who doesn't need to text you every hour to prove the relationship is working.

Checking too often doesn't make you smarter, richer, or safer. It just makes you tired. Investing isn't about winning the day—it's about winning the decades. And the less time you spend staring at numbers, the more likely you are to let those decades do their job.

The Freedom of Boring Wealth

Most people think wealth has to look exciting. They imagine high-stakes trades, dramatic stock picks, and adrenaline-pumping moments where fortunes are made or lost in seconds. That image sells movies and headlines, but it's terrible for real life. The truth is that boring wealth—the kind built through steady, automated investing—is the kind that buys freedom. It doesn't flash, it doesn't brag, but it lets you live the life you want without money constantly breathing down your neck.

Boring wealth starts with consistency. You put money into broad index funds or ETFs month after month, and you don't chase the latest craze. It's the financial equivalent of eating a balanced diet instead of crash dieting. At first, it looks unremarkable. There's no big drama, no thrilling highs, no devastating crashes. But over the years, this steady approach compounds into something remarkable. Suddenly the numbers on your account are bigger than you expected, and you realize that what felt dull was actually powerful.

The beauty of boring wealth is that it doesn't demand your attention every day. You don't have to check balances constantly, you don't have to follow every headline, and you don't have to argue with your cousin about the newest crypto. Your money is on autopilot, quietly multiplying while you focus on your career, your family, or just living your life. The very lack of excitement is what makes it sustainable. You stick with it not because it thrills you, but because it doesn't exhaust you.

This calm approach also protects you from the emotional traps that wreck investors. If you're not chasing drama, you're less likely to panic when the market dips. You know your system is built for the long haul, so you ride out volatility instead of reacting to it. You don't need to be the smartest or boldest person in the room—you just need to be the one who keeps going. That persistence beats brilliance almost every time. Boring wealth wins because it doesn't quit.

The emotional payoff is enormous. Picture the peace of knowing your bills are covered, your retirement is on track, and you don't have to hustle endlessly just to stay afloat. That's what boring wealth buys: space to breathe. It gives you time with your family, the freedom to pursue projects you actually care about, and the confidence that you won't be derailed by the next financial storm. In the end, it's not about the thrill of investing—it's about the life it enables.

Some of the wealthiest and most secure people never made a splash on Wall Street. They lived below their means, invested steadily, and let time and compounding do the work. Their accounts grew quietly in the background while their lives moved forward. That's the real magic: wealth that doesn't consume you. You don't work for it every day—it works for you.

The freedom of boring wealth is that it removes money from the list of things you constantly worry about. Once your system is in place, money becomes background noise instead of a daily obsession. That quiet is priceless. It's not glamorous, but it's real. It's what allows you to sleep well at night, wake up without panic, and move through your days knowing the future is under control. That's the kind of wealth that matters—the kind that doesn't demand attention but delivers freedom all the same.

From Beginner to Confident Investor

Finishing this journey feels less like crossing a finish line and more like stepping out of training wheels. You've learned the basics, set up your accounts, dodged the scams, built your starter portfolio, and automated your progress. You're not a Wall Street hotshot, and that's the point—you're something better: a confident investor who can calmly steer through the noise. Confidence in money doesn't come from knowing every term in the finance dictionary. It comes from clarity, from having a plan, and from sticking with it no matter how messy the headlines get.

Confidence shows up in small ways first. You'll notice it when someone at work starts bragging about their stock picks, and you don't feel that pang of envy. You'll see it when your account dips and you don't panic, because you know volatility is part of the process. You'll feel it at family dinners when your uncle drops his latest "surefire" scheme and you can smile instead of squirm. What you've built is the muscle of calm. And that calm, over time, is worth more than any hot tip.

The transition from beginner to confident investor is less about learning new tricks and more about trusting the ones you already know. At this point, you've seen how compounding works, you understand how to avoid hype, and you've practiced patience. You don't need to chase every opportunity that pops up. You can now ask, "Does this fit my plan?" instead of "Am I missing out?" That single shift—from chasing to choosing—is the hallmark of confidence.

Part of this confidence is knowing what questions you can answer yourself. Before, you might have Googled everything, drowning in jargon. Now you can decode the basics on your own. You can look at an investment option and tell if it's a scam. You can explain index funds in plain English. You can sketch out your portfolio allocation without breaking a sweat. These small victories accumulate into something powerful: financial fluency. You've moved from nodding along to actually leading the conversation.

Confidence doesn't mean arrogance. It doesn't mean you'll never make mistakes. It means you have the humility to stick with what works and the perspective to ignore the noise. The market will still crash sometimes. There will still be headlines screaming about disasters or booms. But instead of reacting with fear or greed, you'll react with patience. You'll remember that you've built a system, and the system works precisely because it's boring and consistent. That trust in your process is confidence in action.

The emotional payoff is enormous. You're no longer in survival mode with money. You're not just reacting—you're directing. You've built a path where your wealth grows quietly in the background, and that frees you to focus on life in the foreground. Confidence in investing isn't about feeling invincible. It's about knowing you don't have to constantly worry. The weight lifts, and you realize you've created stability in a world that thrives on uncertainty.

This chapter is your graduation moment. You're not done learning—there's always more out there—but you've crossed the line from anxious beginner to steady hand. That shift changes how you see not just money, but yourself. You're capable, you're consistent, and you've built a relationship with money that serves your goals instead of undermining them. That's the power of confidence. It doesn't scream, it doesn't boast—it just stays steady, compounding quietly in the background while your life opens up in the foreground.

The Graduation Moment

Graduation in investing doesn't come with a diploma or a cap and gown. It comes with a feeling, a shift you notice in yourself when you realize money no longer terrifies you the way it once did. The Graduation Moment is subtle but powerful. It's the day you catch yourself answering a money question with confidence instead of hesitation. It's the moment you recognize you're not just surviving with money—you're directing it, shaping it, and making it serve your goals.

This transition happens quietly. It isn't announced with bells or fireworks. It shows up when you glance at your account and feel calm instead of anxious. It's there when a friend brags about the latest stock tip and you don't feel pressure to join in. It's the steady confidence of knowing your system is working in the background, compounding away while you go about your life. That calm is your certificate of progress.

The Graduation Moment is about control. Not the frantic kind of control where you check balances ten times a day, but the quiet control of having a plan. You know where your money goes every month, you know why it's invested the way it is, and you know you don't need to chase every new opportunity that pops up. The fear of doing it wrong has faded, replaced by the clarity of doing it consistently. That shift from fear to calm is what marks you as someone who has truly leveled up.

Think about how far you've come. At the beginning, investing probably felt like a casino or a foreign language. You worried about scams, you wrestled with the jargon, you doubted whether you could ever really understand it. Now, you've built habits that protect you from those traps. You've automated contributions, learned to avoid hype, and created a portfolio that grows in line with your goals. The transformation isn't just financial—it's emotional. You've gone from being on the outside of money conversations to being someone who can lead them.

Confidence doesn't mean you've learned everything. It means you've learned enough to trust yourself. There will still be market crashes, unexpected expenses, and moments of doubt. But instead of reacting with panic, you'll respond with patience. You'll remind yourself that downturns are temporary, that compounding requires time, and that your system is designed to handle storms. That resilience is the real test of graduation. It's not about avoiding mistakes—it's about handling them without losing sight of the bigger picture.

The emotional payoff of this moment is freedom. You've proven to yourself that you're capable of managing your money without constant stress. You can sit at dinner tables, in work meetings, or across from financial professionals and know you're not being talked over or tricked. You can nod, ask questions, or even push back when advice doesn't fit your plan. You've gained the kind of confidence that changes not only your finances but your sense of self. You're no longer intimidated—you're empowered.

This is your graduation moment. You don't need applause to validate it. The evidence is in the calm you carry and the consistency you practice. The shift is permanent because it's rooted in habits, not hype. You've earned the right to see yourself as an investor—not a gambler, not a spectator, but a steady builder of wealth. That identity, once claimed, becomes a part of you. And with it, you step into the next stage of your financial life, where clarity and calm become your most valuable assets.

Questions You Can Now Answer Yourself

Confidence in investing isn't measured by how many complicated charts you can analyze or how many acronyms you can rattle off. It's measured by the questions you can finally answer without running to Google, without texting a friend, and without doubting yourself. This stage is where you realize that what once felt like advanced finance is now well within your grasp. You may not have all the answers, but you have enough to guide yourself without fear of making a catastrophic mistake.

The first kind of question you can now answer is the basic "what should I do with this extra money?" Before, you might have shoved it into a savings account or let it sit in checking because you weren't sure. Now, you know that consistent contributions to your index fund or retirement account are the right move. You don't wonder if you should chase a hot tip or wait for the perfect moment—you know steady beats sporadic, and time in the market beats timing the market.

Another common question is, "Am I falling for a scam?" Early on, every investment pitch sounded legitimate, and it was easy to be dazzled by confident language or complex promises. Now, you have the tools to sniff out the nonsense. You can look at an offer and quickly identify red flags—guaranteed returns, pressure to act immediately, or a lack of transparency. Instead of panic or confusion, you now respond with calm skepticism. That skill alone saves you from losing thousands and gives you the relief of knowing you're no longer an easy target.

You can also answer the question, "Am I diversified enough?" Once upon a time, diversification was just a buzzword. Now you understand it in plain

English. You know that by owning a total stock market index fund, you're already holding tiny slices of thousands of companies. You don't need to clutter your account with endless funds that overlap. You can explain to yourself—and to others—why one or two broad funds are more powerful than a laundry list of fancy products.

Even taxes, the subject that makes most beginners break into a sweat, become less intimidating. You may not be a tax expert, but you can answer the core question: "How does this affect me?" You know retirement accounts like IRAs or 401(k)s come with tax advantages. You know the basics of capital gains versus ordinary income. Instead of freezing up, you have a working framework. That knowledge turns tax season from a panic-inducing mystery into a routine part of the plan.

One of the most satisfying questions you can now answer is, "Am I on track?" At the beginning, the future felt abstract. Retirement was a vague, distant concept. Now, you can run a quick mental check. You know how much you're contributing, you understand the power of compounding, and you've seen how steady growth adds up. You don't need exact projections to know you're moving in the right direction. That reassurance changes everything. It replaces anxiety with momentum.

This new ability doesn't mean you'll never seek advice again. A confident investor still asks questions and keeps learning. But the difference is that you no longer feel helpless. You're not searching blindly—you're evaluating. You're not absorbing advice without filter—you're weighing it against what you know. That shift is subtle but profound. You've moved from student to practitioner, from overwhelmed to capable.

The emotional beat here is empowerment. Every question you can now answer for yourself chips away at fear and builds a sense of mastery. You don't need to know everything to feel confident—you just need to know enough to trust your process. That trust is the foundation of long-term success, and now it's yours to carry forward.

The Checklist of Calm

Confidence isn't about memorizing every rule of finance—it's about having a system you can return to whenever doubt creeps in. That's where the Checklist of Calm comes in. It's not a rigid set of instructions you must follow step by step. It's a mental framework, a grounding ritual you can lean on whenever the markets wobble, headlines scream, or life throws surprises. This checklist is proof that you don't need to react emotionally, because you've already built a plan that carries you forward.

The first element of the checklist is clarity. Are your automatic contributions still flowing? If the answer is yes, then you know the machine is running. Money is being funneled into your portfolio every month, compounding in the background. That clarity alone often dissolves anxiety, because it reminds you that progress is happening even if the numbers on the screen are dipping this week. The habit is intact, and the habit is what creates wealth.

The next step is alignment. Are your allocations still matching your chosen plan? If your target was sixty percent stocks and forty percent bonds, has that drifted? This isn't about perfection, but about keeping yourself in the ballpark. If you're still aligned with your original intent, you can relax. If not, your annual rebalancing ritual will handle it. Either way, you're not drifting aimlessly. You know your portfolio is set up for the long haul.

The checklist also includes perspective. Markets crash. They always have, and they always will. But zooming out shows the steady upward climb over decades. Your job isn't to avoid every downturn—it's to stay invested through them. When panic tempts you, glance at history. See how every crash has eventually recovered. That perspective is what keeps you from making short-term decisions that damage long-term results.

Another checkpoint is simplicity. Are you complicating your investments unnecessarily? Adding new funds because of fear or greed? The calm investor knows that fewer moving parts mean less stress. Returning to simplicity—one or two broad index funds, maybe a bond fund—is often the fastest way to regain peace of mind. Complexity creates confusion, and confusion fuels fear. Simplicity, on the other hand, reinforces control.

One more item belongs on the list: time horizon. Ask yourself, "When do I actually need this money?" If the answer is twenty years from now, why stress about a dip this week? Keeping your time horizon front and center shrinks today's drama into perspective. Suddenly a five percent drop looks trivial compared to decades of compounding ahead. This single reminder is often enough to turn panic into patience.

The Checklist of Calm doesn't need to be written on paper, though some investors find comfort in that. It's more about the mindset. Whenever you feel rattled, walk through it. Are my contributions consistent? Is my portfolio aligned? Do I have perspective? Am I keeping it simple? Do I remember my time horizon? If the answers are yes, then you're fine. You don't need to do anything. The calm comes not from control over the market, but from control over your own process.

The emotional beat here is reassurance. The checklist proves to you that you're not lost, you're not flailing, and you're not at the mercy of chaos. You're following a framework built for storms. That realization is what separates the anxious beginner from the confident investor. You can't control the waves, but you've built a boat strong enough to ride them. And every time you walk through this checklist, you remind yourself that you're not guessing anymore—you're investing with calm, deliberate intent.

What's Next (Optional Nerd Stuff)

Reaching this point doesn't mean your learning stops. It just means you've built a strong foundation that will carry you through most of your financial life. But for those who feel the itch to go further, there's a whole universe of optional nerd stuff waiting beyond the basics. This isn't required homework—it's more like elective classes. You can ignore them and still succeed brilliantly. But if you're curious, diving into these areas can be both fun and rewarding, as long as you remember that your core system—steady contributions, simple allocations, and patience—remains untouched.

One of the most common next steps is real estate. Some investors like the idea of owning property, whether it's a rental house, a small apartment building, or even short-term rentals. Real estate has the appeal of being tangible—you can touch it, paint it, and brag about it at parties. It also offers income streams through rent and potential appreciation over time. But real estate comes with headaches too: maintenance, vacancies, repairs, and the occasional nightmare tenant. For some, those challenges are worth it. For others, it's easier to stick with REITs (real estate investment trusts), which are basically real estate packaged into a stock you can buy like any other. Both paths give exposure to the housing market, but one requires plungers and paintbrushes, while the other just needs a click.

Another avenue is starting or investing in small businesses. Maybe you've always dreamed of owning a coffee shop, launching a side hustle, or putting money into a friend's startup. Business ownership can be thrilling and profitable, but it's also one of the riskiest bets. Unlike index funds, small businesses fail all the time. The upside is high, but so is the stress. If you go this route, it's best to treat it as a passion project first and an investment second. The key is never to risk money you can't afford to lose. For some, this outlet scratches an itch that index funds never will—it's a chance to be creative, to build something new, and maybe, just maybe, to strike gold.

Advanced investing also includes exploring asset classes beyond stocks and bonds. Some investors like to dabble in commodities, currencies, or alternative assets like gold, art, or even wine. These niches can feel exotic and exciting, but they rarely beat the simple strategy of broad diversification. The danger is getting lost in the weeds and mistaking complexity for sophistication. Remember, sophistication in investing isn't about jargon—it's about results. Still, if you enjoy learning, experimenting with a small slice of your portfolio in these areas can be educational and engaging, as long as you keep the bulk of your wealth in your reliable, boring core.

For the truly curious, there's also the world of financial optimization. This means digging into tax strategies, charitable giving methods, and retirement withdrawal plans. These are areas where the details matter, and getting them right can save or earn you thousands. It's not about gambling on hot tips but about learning how the system works so you can keep more of what you earn. Many investors hire professionals at this stage to fine-tune their strategies, not because they're helpless, but because they know the value of expert input once the stakes are higher.

The emotional key here is choice. You don't have to pursue any of these advanced topics to succeed. You can stop right here, with your automated contributions and balanced portfolio, and know you're on the path to financial independence. But if you want to keep learning, the doors are open. Optional nerd stuff can deepen your understanding, keep you engaged, and make the journey more interesting. Just remember: the foundation never changes. The basics are enough. Everything else is spice, not the meal. Explore if you want, ignore if you don't—the point is that you now have the confidence to decide for yourself, and that's the real win.

The Relief Payoff

At the end of this journey, the greatest reward isn't just the number on your account balance. It's the feeling that comes with it—the relief payoff. Relief is underrated in a culture obsessed with excitement and drama. Everyone wants the thrill of a big win, but what actually changes your life is the quiet knowledge that you're secure, that you've built a system, and that money has stopped being a constant source of stress. That's what this entire book has been working toward: not just wealth, but peace.

The relief payoff is waking up in the morning and realizing you no longer panic about bills or retirement. It's checking your bank account and feeling calm instead of dread. It's the confidence to walk past a flashy stock headline and not feel the pull of fear or envy. The payoff isn't about feeling richer than your neighbor—it's about feeling in control of your own story. You no longer wonder if you're doing enough, because you know your system is running in the background, building steadily every day.

Think back to where you started. Maybe you felt investing was just gambling in disguise. Maybe you carried memories of money disasters, like chasing hot tips or falling for hype. Maybe you distrusted the whole system, assuming it was designed to trick you. Now compare that to where you stand today. You understand the basics. You've learned to avoid scams. You've built a portfolio that fits your life. You've automated it so it keeps growing without constant supervision. That shift, from fear to calm, is the essence of the relief payoff.

This relief isn't passive—it's empowering. When you're no longer paralyzed by money anxiety, you gain the freedom to make better choices in every other area of life. You can switch careers without terror. You can start a family or a business without being consumed by financial panic. You can give generously because you know your own future is secure. Relief isn't about settling—it's about opening space for growth. The stress that once drained you is replaced by energy you can now use to live the life you actually want.

The relief payoff also shows up in relationships. Money is one of the biggest sources of tension between couples, families, and even friends. When you've built a calm, reliable system, those arguments shrink. You can have conversations about goals instead of fights about mistakes. You can talk with your partner about shared dreams instead of shared fears. You can set an example for kids, showing them that money doesn't have to be chaos—it can be simple, steady, and empowering.

The emotional anchor of this chapter is closure. You've walked through fear, confusion, and temptation. You've learned to laugh at hype, to trust in compounding, and to find peace in boring wealth. Now you're here, at the point where money no longer runs the show. That sense of relief is the true treasure. It doesn't sparkle, but it shines in the way your shoulders feel lighter, your sleep comes easier, and your decisions feel clearer. It's not a jackpot moment—it's a lifelong reward.

The relief payoff proves that wealth isn't just about having more. It's about worrying less. You've built a system that works without demanding constant attention, and that system is now your safety net and springboard. You can step forward with clarity, knowing your future is secure. That's the real win. Not the thrill of risky bets or the rush of lucky breaks, but the deep, quiet satisfaction of knowing you've outsmarted fear, reclaimed your time, and built a foundation strong enough to carry you anywhere you want to go.

Money as a Team Sport

The final piece of the puzzle is realizing that money doesn't live in isolation. It's not just your private game—it's a team sport. The way you handle it affects your partner, your family, and even your closest friends. You could build wealth alone, but sharing the journey makes it stronger. Talking about money openly, without shame or secrecy, is one of the most powerful habits you can build. It transforms finances from a source of tension into a shared tool for building the life you want together.

Think about couples who never talk about money. The silence usually hides fear, insecurity, or resentment. One person might be quietly worried about bills while the other assumes everything is fine. One might be investing steadily while the other secretly racks up debt. That gap grows until it explodes into arguments. But when money becomes a shared conversation, it shifts from a hidden stressor to a mutual plan. Suddenly, you're not fighting each other—you're fighting the problem together.

Here's how it starts. You don't need a spreadsheet or a lecture. You just need a simple conversation that says, "Here's what I'm doing, here's what I want, and I'd like us to figure this out together." That script works for couples, siblings, even close friends. It strips money of its taboo status and reframes it as part of life, like health or career. The first talk may feel awkward, but once the door is open, it gets easier. The goal isn't perfect agreement—it's alignment. You may have different styles, but you can share the same direction.

The benefits ripple out. When you and your partner talk about money, you reduce the hidden anxieties that creep into every other part of the relationship. You stop arguing about small purchases because you both understand the bigger plan. You can dream together—vacations, a home, retirement—without those dreams being clouded by unspoken fears. Even disagreements become healthier, because you're debating choices within a shared framework instead of lobbing accusations from separate corners.

Money as a team sport also applies to families. Parents who model calm, consistent investing pass on confidence to their kids. Instead of inheriting fear or confusion, the next generation learns that money is manageable. Friends benefit too. When you share your approach, you give them permission to rethink theirs. You don't have to preach—you just have to be an example of what calm, consistent investing looks like.

There's also power in accountability. When you talk openly, you create gentle pressure to stick with your plan. It's harder to skip contributions or panic-sell when someone else knows the strategy you agreed on. That accountability isn't about control—it's about support. Just like training for a marathon, having someone on the journey keeps you steady when you feel tempted to quit.

The emotional beat here is unity. Money stops being a wedge and becomes a bridge. You realize you're not alone in this, and that realization lightens the load. The confidence you've built individually expands when it's shared. It becomes less about "my plan" and more about "our future." That shift cements the journey. Wealth is no longer a lonely climb but a shared path, and walking it together makes the destination even sweeter.

With this final step, you've moved from fear to calm, from confusion to clarity, and from isolation to unity. Money is no longer the silent enemy in the background—it's the quiet teammate supporting everything you want to build. That's the ultimate sign of mastery: not just securing your own future, but creating stability and confidence that extend to the people you care about most.

You No Longer Need to Gamble

You started this journey with fear in your gut and doubt in your head. Investing looked like a casino, a scam, or a secret language you'd never be fluent in. Now, you've built something different: a system that works quietly in the background, a mindset that resists panic, and a confidence that comes from clarity. The real reward isn't just money—it's freedom from the constant weight of worry. You no longer need to gamble, chase hype, or rely on luck. You've learned how to turn investing into something boring, steady, and powerful, and that boring engine is what builds a rich life.

This isn't the end of your financial story. It's the beginning of a calmer one. As your wealth grows, so will your choices—about where to live, how to work, and what dreams to chase. The system you've created is your foundation. It will carry you through storms and give you the freedom to focus on the things money can't buy: time, relationships, and meaning. That's the real win. That's the future you've built.

Don't miss out!

Visit the website below and you can sign up to receive emails whenever Ryan Papadopoulos publishes a new book. There's no charge and no obligation.

https://books2read.com/r/B-A-FNUUE-EAWQH

BOOKS 2 READ

Connecting independent readers to independent writers.

Did you love *Investing for Beginners: Safe, Stress-Free Wealth Building with Index Funds Without Risky Stock Gambling*? Then you should read *How to Use AI for Work, Money and Productivity: Smart Tools and Prompts to Save Time, Earn More and Stay Sane*[1] by Leila Brandt!

[2]

Think AI is only for coders, tech bros, or Silicon Valley insiders? Think again.

How to Use AI (Even If You're Not a Tech Person) is your no-nonsense guide to using artificial intelligence to boost your productivity, simplify your workflow, and get ahead — without needing a computer science degree or learning to "prompt engineer" like a robot whisperer.

This book is built for real people: business owners, freelancers, students, creatives, side hustlers, job seekers, and anyone who's curious about AI but feels totally lost when it comes to actually using it. Inside, you'll get hands-on help with how to write better, think faster, brainstorm smarter, and automate the boring stuff — all with free or low-cost AI tools you can start using today.

---

1. https://books2read.com/u/boJGLV
2. https://books2read.com/u/boJGLV

You'll learn how to use ChatGPT, Claude, Perplexity, and other AI tools even if you've never used them before. You'll find out how to write better emails in seconds, draft blog posts without burnout, summarize long documents, prep for job interviews, level up your resume, build content calendars, generate creative ideas, and more — all without getting stuck in tech overwhelm.

This isn't another hype-driven book that overpromises and under-explains. It's a practical, plain-English manual that shows you exactly how to make AI work for you — even if you're not "good with computers."

Whether you want to save time, grow your business, write faster, or just stop staring at the blinking cursor, this book will show you how to plug into the power of AI without selling your soul to the machine.

www.ingramcontent.com/pod-product-compliance
Lightning Source LLC
LaVergne TN
LVHW100332210926
848480LV00003B/1310